Home and hearth mar
It's where we make p.
has drawn up a map we can read and follow, so that
arrive at the goal, together with our families.

—Dr. Scott Hahn
Founder and President of
the St. Paul Center for Biblical Theology,
Bestselling author and speaker

Katie Warner is right: our times call for strong spiritual leadership, especially within the home. When husbands and wives discover that they have a mission from God, with unique complementary roles, and that He provides the grace to fulfill those roles together, then the Church in our day will bear much fruit. May this book help many of our families go forward confidently and joyfully, taking up God's plan for marriage.

—Most Reverend Thomas J. Olmsted
Bishop of Phoenix

The family is a work of art; it will not create itself. Great artists sacrifice everything for their masterpiece—they fix every mistake and apply each brush stroke with love and care, creating a treasure for the ages. Should we treat our families any differently? Husbands and wives, dads and moms need skills and determined efforts for their families to thrive. Warner provides guidelines and encouragement to assist parents in taking up their leadership responsibilities to create and nurture a masterpiece for heaven. Read this book now and your children will thank you later.

—Steve Ray
Author of St. John's Gospel,
Upon This Rock, *and* Crossing the Tiber

In *Head & Heart*, Katie Warner gives this generation of Catholic parents a valuable tool—not just for parenting their children but also for leading them to holiness. What an important vision for every family to have, and this book gives practical examples of how to do it! I think Pope St. John Paul the Great captured the importance of this mission when he said, "As the family goes, so goes the nation, and so goes the whole world in which we live."

—Tom Monaghan
*Founder of Ave Maria University & School of Law
and Founder of Legatus*

We Catholics have the Bible, the sacraments, the Catechism, and the wisdom of the saints. So why do so many of us navigate through life like we don't have a map? In *Head & Heart*, Katie Warner not only shows that strong leaders come from strong families, which are built upon strong marriages, she offers hope to those who grew up in dysfunctional family environments where the head and the heart have been separated. As an antidote, this fine book normalizes holiness for each family member and shows how within reach it is. The only one holding you back is you.

—Patrick Coffin
*Host of Catholic Answers Live and author of
Sex Au Naturel: What It Is
and Why It's Good For Your Marriage;
Co-founder of Immaculata Pictures*

This is a most welcome guide for any parents who are serious about strengthening their families and growing with their children in the spiritual life. Parents are the first and most important teachers of their children. Katie Warner and those Catholic parents who have contributed to this book give indispensable and reassuring guidance to parents in their work of becoming spiritual leaders. At this time, when family life is threatened in so many ways, do your family a big favor and read this book.

—Bishop Michael Sheridan
Bishop of Colorado Springs

It is one thing to tell young people that they need to raise their family Catholic. It's another thing to show them how. Katie has given us clear direction on how your home can become a school of love and the place where wisdom and holiness are learned. I would recommend *Head & Heart* to every engaged couple and suggest that those who have been married for a while pause and gain new insight.

—Jeff Cavins
Creator of the Great Adventure Bible Timeline

The wisdom in *Head & Heart* will certainly help others to form fine families in these challenging times. As a priest who has been involved with marriage prep for a quarter of a century, I intend to give this book as a wedding gift to the couples I prepare for their sacrament and vocation.

—Fr. John Riley
Chaplain of the Augustine Institute, Denver

I believe the very best books are born in a moment of urgent need. After an intense and illuminating conversation with her husband about being the Catholic leader of their home, Katie saw the need for a practical guide for creating authentic Catholic homes and stronger families. The result is this excellent book. *Head & Heart* is a true gift to everyone in the Church, regardless if you are single or married, a new couple, or great-grandparents. If you desire to build a stronger marriage and a Catholic home built on an excellent foundation, read *Head & Heart*. You will be glad you did!

—Randy Hain
Author of Journey to Heaven:
A Road Map for Catholic Men;
Special Children, Blessed Fathers: Encouragement for
Fathers of Children with Special Needs;
The Integrated Catholic Life *eMagazine*

Katie Warner brings to light some of the acute issues plaguing families in our modern society and offers practical insights on how to deal with them. We should never forget that the family is the foundation and soul of society. In this book, Katie demonstrates why and how we can continue with this indispensable task of strengthening our families.

—Fr. Henry Atem
Pastor of St. George Catholic Church,
Archdiocese of Atlanta

Today, it's not unusual for young Catholic parents to find themselves deficient in the knowledge of how to create a faith-filled atmosphere for their growing families. Katie Warner has combined her own experiences and insights with those of other Catholic parents to provide a complete book of instructions, inspiration, and lots of great ideas for immersing families in a Catholic culture. It's practical, uplifting, and leaves no stone unturned.

—Patti Maguire Armstrong
Author, speaker, and Catholic mother of ten

What better way to encourage the spiritual leadership within families than to share the wisdom of those who are in the trenches and walking the talk? *Head & Heart* is a great tool to help families and individuals in their role as formators of future disciples.

—Bishop Sam Jacobs
Bishop Emeritus of Houma-Thibodaux

Head & Heart: Becoming Spiritual Leaders for Your Family is a great tool for husbands and wives and a special gift to families. Raising faith-filled children within healthy Catholic families is a challenge in light of all the distractions and influences of our culture. I welcome support for our families that is soundly based on the Scriptures and Catholic teaching.

—Monsignor Peter Rau
Pastor of St. Peter Chanel Catholic Church,
Archdiocese of Atlanta

This book is for anyone who wants the Catholic faith to play a stronger role in marriage and family life, but isn't sure, practically, what to do. With a wide range of practical advice and stories from people of all ages and family sizes, *Head & Heart* will help you take small steps toward building a vibrant Catholic identity in your home.

—Dr. Edward Sri
Author of Queen Mother:
A Biblical Theology of Mary's Queenship
and Mystery of the Kingdom: On the Gospel of Matthew

HEAD &
Heart

BECOMING SPIRITUAL
LEADERS FOR YOUR FAMILY

HEAD&
Heart

BECOMING SPIRITUAL
LEADERS FOR YOUR FAMILY

KATIE WARNER

FOREWORD BY
BISHOP JAMES D. CONLEY

EMMAUS
ROAD
PUBLISHING

Steubenville, Ohio
www.emmausroad.org

Emmaus Road Publishing
1468 Parkview Circle
Steubenville, Ohio 43952

Library of Congress Control Number: 2015945174
ISBN: 978-1-941447-28-4

Cover design and layout by Mairead Cameron

FOR RAYMOND

Table of Contents

Foreword

We are created for family life. To be created in God's image is to be made for family life—the sharing of fruitful love. Since the time of creation itself, God has destined men and women to share the unity of family life and to share in the life-giving love of the Trinity.

The Blessed Trinity is the communion of the Father, the Son, and the Holy Spirit, united by the eternal act of giving and receiving love. Our family life is made in the image of that love and is made to reflect that love in the world.

God reveals Himself to the world through families. In Eden, God revealed His will for the world through a family. Through the family of Abraham, He revealed His law and formed His chosen people. And through the Holy Family, God Himself came into the world, in the Incarnation of Jesus Christ.

The Christian life is inseparable from family life. Even those who are unmarried or have no children are called to spiritual fatherhood and motherhood. We are all adopted sons and daughters of God through baptism. We are brothers and sisters to one another, sons and daughters of Mary, and united in the family of God, the Church of Jesus Christ.

Pope St. John Paul II wrote that, "the family is placed at the center of the great struggle between good and evil, between life and death, between love and all that is opposed to love."

Parents are called to the task of forming the family as a domestic Church rooted in Jesus Christ, which has the Gospel as the source of its means and identity. Cultural opposition to the values of the Gospel makes this task difficult. Today the struggle between good and evil poses particular difficulties for family life.

In civil law the family is being radically redefined—gutted of its basic meaning and of its divinely revealed purpose. Marriage has lost its meaning for many people, becoming a kind of cultural endorsement for social relationships, instead of a lifelong partnership oriented to the procreation and education of children.

In all times, forming children as disciples of Jesus Christ is difficult. But today, when culture has lost much of its connection to the Gospel, Catholic parents must be vigilant proponents of a vision for family life that seems foreign to many of their contemporaries. Catholic parents are called to form their children in faith—to build lifelong disciples of Jesus Christ who know the Lord and love Him entirely.

Parents must witness to the durability and fidelity of marriage when those values have been lost. Parents must celebrate virtue when license has become *de riguer*. Parents must form free and joyful human beings, when most notions of the good life have become subsumed by the "dictatorship of relativism."

But the task of forming authentically Catholic families is the first step to forming an authentically Catholic culture. Without question, the renewal of Christian culture in our country depends on the renewal of Christian families, and the renewal of Christian families requires that couples are committed to leading their families closer to Christ.

Weaving in Scriptural wisdom, the teaching of the Church, and stories of everyday families, *Head & Heart* helps men and women find the joy that comes from saying yes to

God's call to lead and to love their families with intention. In *Head & Heart*, Katie Warner addresses the crisis of spiritual leadership and helps guide couples to become strong servant-leaders for their families.

Many Catholic parents tell me that they are looking for help in forming authentically Catholic culture in their families. Though there is no sure blueprint for that task, Catholic parents can learn from one another. They can learn to bring prayer to the center of family life. They can learn to celebrate the liturgical seasons of the Church. They can learn to help foster holy vocations, and to help develop apostolic fervor for Jesus Christ.

This book contains reflections from Catholic parents on the formation of Catholic family cultures. Each family is unique, and the life of every Catholic home is different. *Head & Heart* offers the "best practices" of Catholic parents who have worked, in many different ways, to become spiritual leaders in their households. Katie not only tells the stories of these modern families trying to adopt a countercultural and lively faith, but also provides practical, implementable tips and strategies for becoming a stronger spiritual leader in one's own home.

I hope that *Head & Heart* will be a resource for every Catholic couple undertaking the task of spiritual leadership. I hope it will spark a renewal of Catholic family culture. And I hope it will bring mothers, fathers, sons, and daughters into a deeper relationship with our mother, the Church, with Christ, our brother, and with God the Father, the great patriarch of every family.

Bishop James Conley
Diocese of Lincoln

Preface

This book began in my husband's tears. It was Holy Thursday, and my husband Raymond and I were on our way home from Mass with our four-month-old son, RJ, sleeping in the back seat of the car. Over the white noise of the car tires against the road, a conversation about learning to live the Catholic faith more intentionally in our home led Ray to vulnerably share his true feelings about his role as a spiritual leader for our family. What he told me inspired this book.

"Katie," he muttered, his voice breaking a little between words. "I know you want me to be the spiritual head of our household. I want that for myself, too. I want to help lead our family to heaven, to be your spiritual anchor, to be the kind of father that our children can learn to grow in holiness from. But, Katie, I don't know *how*."

My husband, like many young Catholics, grew up going to Sunday Mass and saying grace before meals, but to him, the Bible was more of a coffee table adornment than a book to be read, prayed with, and lived. As a teen, his faith didn't extend far beyond going to youth nights at his parish. It was during college that something (or some*one*—the Holy Spirit) sparked a desire in him to learn more about his faith. Ray began reading and learning more about Catholicism, but he still had little observed or lived experience from which to draw *practical* tools for being successful at this massive vocation of spiritual leadership within the family. Now that we were married and had started our family, both of us wanted more. We wanted a guidebook, a game plan to help us become the spiritual head and the spiritual heart of our family that we knew God made us to be. This book was written to help my family and others see what strong spiritual leadership *looks like*, and then customize and implement the characteristics that embody strong leaders in our own home life so we can better love and lead our families toward heaven.

Men and women in the thick of family life with young kids at home, adults with grown children, engaged couples, married men and women without children, and even grandparents can learn something from the stories, ideas, teachings, and strategies in this book and contribute to a gradual but determined rise in Catholic families cultivating an intentional and vibrant Christian culture in the home.

Acknowledgements

It was exciting to watch the Holy Spirit at work throughout the brainstorming, writing, and editing phases of this book. I truly thank God for guiding me to the right people to interview and for unearthing pockets of time during my year as a new mother to bring this whole book together.

I have a profound sense of gratitude for my husband, Raymond, since his vulnerability not only sparked the topic for this book, but his input along the way shaped the entire project. I am thankful that God sent him into my life, as he lovingly deals with my many moments of insanity, sacrifices gallantly for our family, and makes daily steps toward becoming the strong spiritual leader that I knew he could be from the moment I met him. Our firstborn son, Raymond (RJ), who I consider my co-author, as much of the writing occurred during his naps snuggled against my chest in his baby carrier, has an amazing example of faith to follow in his father.

My parents, Tom and Tricia Peterson, were incredible spiritual leaders in my life and in our family growing up, and I would be remiss if I failed to thank them for setting a shining example of what it means to raise a family to follow Christ. My mother has been my primary editor for the past decade, and I am also deeply appreciative of the time she poured into reading and editing this work, too. My parents-in-law, Ray and Michele Warner, in addition to my sisters, Kimberly and Kristina, and siblings-in-law Brian and Rachele, were highly motivating cheerleaders and prayer warriors over the past year, and I have no doubt that their prayers influenced not only the book, but will impact the readers as well.

I have long respected Bishop James Conley, since I first met him in Denver and during the brief time he served as my spiritual director when we both lived there. His clear and bold voice for truth inspires individuals and families to become stronger spiritual leaders, better citizens, and more faithful disciples of Christ. I couldn't imagine a better shepherd and writer to have penned the foreword for this book.

I probably wouldn't have the writing platform that I do if it weren't for Randy Hain and Deacon Mike Bickerstaff of the IntegratedCatholicLife.org giving me my first widespread avenue to share my spiritual musings when I was fresh out of high school with still so much to learn. For years, Randy has encouraged me to write a book, and not only guided me toward Emmaus Road Publishing, but advised me throughout the entire writing process. Randy continues to be one of my greatest advocates and dear friends in the work of evangelization, and I am grateful and undeserving of his mentorship.

For years I have appreciated Emmaus Road's books, which inform and inspire the Catholic laity, and I was thankful to work with the Emmaus Road team on this work.

Finally, every contributor in every chapter of this book has deeply moved and inspired me. Words simply cannot express the gratitude I have for their allowing me and the readers of this book to gaze into the windows of their homes and witness the ways in which they lead their families toward heaven. To each of the men, women, and couples who offered their insights and gave of their time and hearts to me: thank you.

How To Use This Book

Some Things to Consider

Before you begin this book, which I hope will be more of a journey than it will be a reading endeavor, here are a few things to consider:

This is an ideas book. Try out the strategies and ideas that resonate with you and don't get hung up by stories or suggestions you can't relate to or don't see working in your own family (but remain open to reconsidering these ideas later). Think outside the box, brainstorming on your own and with your spouse new ideas and strategies to try to improve on a particular characteristic of your spiritual leadership. Some ideas will stick and others won't, but give the ones you try a fair, intentional, repeated shot.

This book will have the greatest impact if you do it as a team. Try to read this book and incorporate its ideas along with your spouse. However, if for whatever reason you are not able to work with your spouse on your spiritual leadership at this time, you will still see positive results if you work to improve your own role as your family's spiritual head or heart. Also consider teaming up with more accountability and prayer partners, for example, at your parish. You can help encourage one another as you work to better lead your families and help one another troubleshoot along the way.

Adopt strategies incrementally. Incorporate ideas in

this book one small step at a time. Consider focusing on a different spiritual leadership characteristic each month. You can go in order by chapter, or even hone in on the leadership characteristics you most want to improve upon first. When developing new habits, most of us usually experience a honeymoon phase with the new way of life, then a struggle to keep it going, and then, eventually, it becomes second nature. Give yourself time to get there.

Identify yourself as a spiritual leader. It is in our nature to fulfill the roles we find ourselves in. When I tell someone I am a writer, I have a strong desire to write more frequently and to write better, so that I can live up to that title I have for myself. Consider yourself right now to be a spiritual leader, and then take this book as your opportunity to help you live out that role more intentionally.

Look ahead and dream big. Envision the future of your family, led by a strong spiritual head and heart. Dare to believe that you are capable of becoming a family of saints, because "with God, all things are possible" (Mt 19:26).

Focus on the present moment. In dreaming big, don't let yourself get overwhelmed by the end goal. Focus on the present moment, one virtuous choice at a time, one prayer at a time. Every choice to sacrifice our selfishness in a given moment brings us a lot closer to our end goal than we sometimes give it credit for.

Track your progress and schedule checkups. Have regularly scheduled times to pray over your progress with the Lord, in a personal heart-to-heart. Supplement with regular checkups with your spouse to assess your progress, and then offer encouragement and make changes or new plans accordingly.

Concentrate on your family, not on other families. Our social media-saturated culture makes it easy for us to measure ourselves against those around us. Your family has its own unique path to holiness and your spiritual leadership is meant to look different from the examples of those around you. Do not focus on what other leaders or families are doing to the point of self-deprecation or doubt when what you are doing for your family is right and according to God's will.

Don't just think, DO: For this book to matter in your life, you have to actually *do something*. Your life and leadership will remain stagnant if you read this book with the intention of being inspired, but plan to do nothing. Action steps at the end of each chapter make it easy for you to do something that tangibly impacts your spiritual leadership and turns good intentions into reality.

Your Most Important Job

*"God takes pleasure to see you
take your little steps."*
—St. Francis de Sales

What Is Spiritual Leadership, and What Does Spiritual Leadership Look Like?

The common understanding of leadership often focuses on an individual's exertion of power or influence over others. When many of us think of leaders, the president of a country or our boss at work may come to mind. We tend to denote leaders by seniority, title, or the management position they hold within a hierarchy or group of people. Empowerment, insight, impact, influence—these qualities contribute to the *stuff* that makes a leader, but a great leader is so much more.

As Christians, we look to Jesus Christ as the epitome of leadership. Ironically, He wasn't at all what the people of His day expected in a leader. Jesus didn't come bearing a lofty title (at least not an earthly one), yet His influence was profound—and strikingly different. His impact wasn't centered on power or command in the way that kings of His day ruled vast nations or generals led grand armies. His leadership was focused on just the opposite: humble service.

This is the crux of spiritual leadership. Spiritual leadership is *servant* leadership. Authentic spiritual leadership, in imitation of Christ, is less about making a name for yourself and more about ushering those you influence into a deeper relationship with God and helping others become the person God wants them to be, as you become more of the person and leader God desires *you* to be. Spiritual leadership is less about external output and more about internal transformation. Spiritual leaders inspire, giving not just their ideas, but their entire selves to those they serve. "The Son of man came not to be served but to serve, and to give his life as a ransom for many" (Mt 20:28). The irony of the Christian life and spiritual leadership is that real happiness comes from dying to ourselves and living for others. True leaders are less known for their display of physical power and are more often remembered for their model of righteousness.

Whether you realized it or not at the time, when you married your spouse and entered into the sublime adventure of family life, you stepped into your God-given role as the spiritual head—the husband and father—or spiritual heart— the wife and mother—of your family. Pope Pius XI wrote in his encyclical on chaste marriage, *Casti Connubii*, "For if the man is the head, the woman is the heart, and as he occupies the chief place in ruling, so she may and ought to claim for herself the chief place in love" (no. 27). Both the head and the heart channel their complementary masculinity and femininity toward the supreme privilege and responsibility of cooperating with God's grace and using the gifts, talents, and tools He has given them to help lead every person in their family to heaven, becoming "saints"—the title given to those who become the persons that God created them to be.

A strong family relies on the uniqueness of these "head" and "heart" roles. The spiritual head of a family uses the uniquely masculine gifts God has given him to care for his family and draw them closer to Christ. As the spiritual head of his household, a man reflects the role of the heavenly Father. He is not only given the opportunity to beget children in his own image and likeness, but he is tasked with the responsibility of educating his children in faith so that they can grow up to follow and return to their ultimate, *heavenly* Father. The spiritual head oversees the kingdom of his family, provides for the physical needs of his family, disciplines his children (Eph 6:4), and sees that his children bear good fruit in the world (Jn 15:16). He exemplifies the outward focus and expansiveness of God. Most especially, he is called to lay down his life for his bride, the spiritual heart of his family, as Christ lays down his life for His Bride, the Church.

The spiritual head of the family makes up half of this beautiful leadership team that God has brought together to raise saints for His glory. The "helper fit for him" (Gen 2:18)—woman—is the spiritual heart of her family. The spiritual heart of a family uses the uniquely *feminine* gifts God has given her to care for her family and draw them closer to Christ. As the spiritual heart, a woman reflects the prototype of the Mother of God—the exemplary spiritual heart of the whole family of God—by nurturing new life in and outside of her womb, and by tending to, in a special way, the physical *and* spiritual development of her family. As the moral provider of her home, she teaches her family, by word and by example, how to cooperate with God, and she is uniquely sensitive to the dignity of each family member. The spiritual heart sacrifices *within* her flesh for her family, as Fulton Sheen describes in *Three to Get Married*: "Not only her days but her nights, not only her mind but her body, must share in the Calvary of mothering." She exemplifies the abidingness of God, and she radiates grace and the love of the inner life of God to her family. She is visibly and actively receptive to her husband's headship, and helps her family's hearts, as Sheen says, "intertwine and grow together" like vines, so as to draw every member of her family together—closer to Christ and His Church, consecrating them to His service.

Refocusing on Spiritual Leadership in Modern Family Life

In many ways, our culture encourages us to focus on all the wrong things when it comes to family life. At best, it fosters a disordering of priorities. The result has been catastrophic on many modern families and, consequently, on our broader culture and even on the Church.

The statistics of young people abandoning the faith that we read about in online articles and popular papers aren't just numbers. They have faces and names. For more than a decade now, I've watched many of my own friends, classmates, and teenage and young adult relatives abandon their Catholic faith and I'm anxious for the youth exodus from the Church to end. I believe the answer to the youth faith crisis lies in responding to a bigger, overarching crisis: the crisis of spiritual leadership in families.

If wives and husbands, fathers and mothers, become strong spiritual leaders for their families, I am convinced that we would see a new era of vitality in the Church—an explosive energy in the Catholic faithful that the Church has long been yearning for. Our children will grow up to be disciples of Jesus Christ and chip away at the statistics that seem so grim, giving hope to the Church and to the world. The world will look to Catholic families as a central source for the Good News of Jesus Christ, and in inculcating the Gospel effectively within their homes, they will experience the fullness of what family life is meant to be. As the apostolic exhortation *Familiaris Consortio* explains, "The Church is deeply convinced that only by the acceptance of the Gospel are the hopes that man legitimately places in marriage and in the family capable of being fulfilled" (no. 3). There is no better foundation and gift that you can give your family than a faith that stands the test of time.

Maybe you have never really understood what you are called to *do* as a spiritual leader, or perhaps distractions just keep getting in the way of your ability to lead your family with focus and intention. Whatever the reason, if you aren't working on becoming a better spiritual leader for your family, you need to be. This book will help you reprioritize, and teach you how to spiritually lead, restructure the way you lead, or inspire you to stay the course and give you some metrics for seeing how you are doing in your effort to be a spiritual head or heart of the family. God intended that we spend our earthly lives mastering our ability to be strong spiritual leaders for our families, becoming better servant leaders to those closest to us, and then from there, we can use the loving and serving skills that we have learned in the home to bless others.

Inspired by Real People

A few months after Ray and I had our crucial conversation, I started virtually traveling the country, interviewing husbands and wives whom I believe are effectively living out the call to be strong spiritual leaders in the home so that I could share their stories and lessons in this book. These men and women, of varying ages and occupations, with young children, grown children, or no children, are all humbly and intentionally living out their vocations as spiritual heads and hearts. Some of their stories made me laugh or tear up. Others challenged me to think in a different way or to grow. All inspired me to become a better spiritual leader in my own home. No one person or family in this book is perfectly alike in their expressions of spiritual leadership. The way you integrate what you learn in this book into your own family life is also meant to be completely unique, specially tailored and adjusted to fit you, your spouse, and your family's unique charisms, gifts, and spirituality.

What You'll Find in Each Chapter

In the subsequent chapters of this book, you will learn seven characteristics of strong spiritual leaders. Each chapter contains:

- Personal and practical reflections and strategies;
- Church teaching;
- Scriptural wisdom;
- Stories and examples of strong spiritual leaders exhibiting a certain characteristic of leadership in their home;
- Heartfelt advice from one spiritual head (husband/father) or spiritual heart (wife/mother) to you, as the spiritual head or heart of your own family;
- And, finally, leadership action steps. Select one action item at the beginner, intermediate, or advanced level that seems like it could be a good fit for you and your family, or come up with a different, but related action step to try.

The Leadership Characteristic That Ties Them All Together

If you put this book down right now and never pick it up again, please remember this: The most important characteristic that strong spiritual leaders exhibit is their desire to fulfill their vocation to love. Like plants draw energy from the sun, all of the other characteristics mentioned in this book draw their vitality from this ultimate vocation of a spiritual leader: to love—to love God with one's whole heart, mind, soul, and strength and to love one's family with intention and purpose, seeing in each of them a reflection of God. This is what strong spiritual leaders do. They love.

Your most important job in life is to learn to love by becoming a strong spiritual head or heart of your family. If you do this job very well, you will become a saint. The pursuit of holiness as a member and leader of a family is not easy, but we should be awed by the supreme privilege we have of making this journey to heaven with a fallen but beautiful team.

Are you ready to lead? Are you prepared for the passion, meaning, and satisfaction that come with fulfilling your God-given role as the spiritual head or spiritual heart of your family?

Take ownership of your spiritual leadership role now. It's the most important decision you will make in your family life.

Seven Characteristics of Strong Spiritual Leaders

1

They Fulfill Unique, Complementary Roles

"Physical, moral, and spiritual difference and complementarity are oriented toward the goods of marriage and the flourishing of family life."
–Catechism of the Catholic Church, 2333

That Dusty Coffee Table

I'll never forget an unexpectedly boisterous discussion that turned a slow-paced morning at our marriage preparation retreat into an unforgettable one. The prompt about tackling chores according to the rule, "Who dusts the coffee table? Whoever bumps into it first," turned our otherwise quiet group mates into quite the opinionated conversationalists.

One young lady in the group made a particularly provocative observation. "Well, I don't know about your fiancés," she began, "but mine doesn't have an eye for dusty coffee tables." She elaborated, "That theory sounds pretty dreamy, but in reality I don't think it works. When I bump into the coffee table, I can't help but see the gobs of puffy dirt polluting the air right in front of me. But when *he* bumps into it, he is mysteriously blind to the cloud of dust rising into the air." Everybody at the table nodded hesitantly. Maybe she had a point.

The conversation about that dusty coffee table nagged at me from that day on. For me, the dusty table eventually became my mental symbol for anything that highlighted the different vantage points from which my husband and I viewed and lived out our unique roles in marriage.

My husband and I naturally found ourselves falling into certain patterns in the way we collaboratively carried out different responsibilities of our everyday living. But soon, a gray area began to emerge: our spiritual lives. We knew that we each had a unique, yet complementary role to play in spiritual leadership in the home, but we couldn't explain with clarity what those roles looked like.

What we wanted was to be confident in the vocations of spiritual headship and spiritual heartship that God called us to when we entered into marriage and family life together. What spiritual responsibilities should my husband oversee? Which spiritual duties should I make my priority as a wife and mother? How do other families fulfill their unique, complementary roles as spiritual heads and hearts?

Head and Heart

A family begins with the joining of a husband and a wife, a spiritual head and a spiritual heart. Just like in the human body, the head and the heart do totally different things, yet both make vital contributions to the body—in this case, the family—as a whole. Try to imagine existing without your head or surviving without your heart! A healthy, living body needs both, and a family that desires to be spiritually healthy and strong needs the same thing: a thriving spiritual head, the husband and father, and a flourishing spiritual heart, the wife and mother.

Our culture today often fights the distinctions between

men and women, between the head and the heart of the family. But families thrive when they are led by a mother and a father, who both bring unique things to the table. Contrary to secular opinion, mothers and fathers cannot easily fulfill one another's roles if they so desire. As Christians, we know better. We know that the God-designed differences between men and women contribute to the enrichment of family life.

"In today's world there is an impression that men and women are the same," explained Greg Willits, Catholic author, radio show host and a diocesan director of evangelization and family life ministries. "A man and a woman are *equal* in the eyes of God, but they are not the *same*." Greg believes that it can be easy to take the false mindset of "sameness" into spiritual leadership as well. But he and his wife, Jennifer, a podcaster and author, see things differently, recognizing the unique talents that they each bring to their leadership roles in the family.

"I present a stronger side of the faith," Greg described. "Jennifer presents a softer side of the faith—not weaker, but softer." For Jennifer, this softer side is vital for spiritually leading their five children—four boys and a girl.

"There are things that women see that sometimes fathers don't see—they see through their hearts and empathize with their children," Jennifer elaborated. "I can tell when one kid is hurting or feels pushed aside. These are opportunities for me to spiritually lead them. It is important for me to respond to those moments with a heart-to-heart connection, but they also need that strength that only fathers can bring."

Greg works to provide that strength to his family, by capitalizing on his God-given masculinity and drawing energy from his own relationship with God. "I think the best thing I can do in terms of spiritual leadership is to set the precedent of respect and honor of the mother in the home," Greg noted. "Also, to set the precedent of prayer,

Mass attendance, and living out our faith as the 'main thing.' Every morning, I get my coffee and grab my Bible, and I sit and pray. The kids know that I do that every day. A father must model prayer and a relationship with Jesus Christ for everyone in the family."

Ultimately, Greg and Jennifer recognize their unique roles as being complementary in their task of working as a team to nurture and grow their family's faith. "We are subordinate to one another in each other's strengths," Greg acknowledged. Perhaps, most importantly, they are there for each other in times of weakness, too. "Sometimes, one of us will be weak for whatever reason—emotionally, spiritually, physically—and the other one at that time is stronger, and I appreciate that God gives a grace to one of us to be able to lift the other up."

The Willits believe that their tasks of being the spiritual head and spiritual heart of their family depend on building a strong trust in Jesus, the definitive Head of the Church and of every family in it. "We often fear that we are going to mess it up somehow," Jennifer admitted. "I have wrestled with the fear that I'm not good enough. How could I possibly fulfill my role of spiritual leadership well, in a way that is pleasing to God? The good news is that being a spiritual head or heart of the household is something that God will equip you for. You can do this, provided you do one thing: trust Jesus."

Made to Complement

As Greg and Jennifer demonstrate, God created men and women to complement one another, which works to our advantage in our spiritual and family lives. If we, as married couples, can capitalize on this complementarity, we will become better spiritual leaders by working in conjunction with our God-given, natural inclinations to lead our families in uniquely masculine or feminine ways.

Pope St. John Paul II sagely wrote in 1995 to the United Nations World Conference on Women, "Women and men have been called by the Creator to live in profound communion with one another, with reciprocal knowledge and giving of self, acting together for the common good with the complementary characteristics of that which is feminine and masculine."

These complementary characteristics extend beyond the purely physical to the spiritual as well. *The Catechism of the Catholic Church* explains:

> Physical, moral, and spiritual difference and complementarity are oriented toward the goods of marriage and the flourishing of family life. The harmony of the couple and of society depends in part on the way in which the complementarity, needs, and mutual support between the sexes are lived out. (CCC 2333)

Dietrich von Hildebrand, a prominent twentieth-century Catholic philosopher and theologian, masterfully argues for this unique complementarity in his lectures and writings. In his book *Marriage: The Mystery of Faithful Love*, von Hildebrand writes:

> Marital love—involving the gift of one's own person . . . in which the whole personality of the beloved is grasped mysteriously as a unity in spite of all outer obstacles—can exist only between two types of the spiritual person, the male and the female, as only between them can this complementary character be found.

He further points out that the dissimilarity, yet complementarity, between men and women allows for "deeper penetration into the soul of the other," which, of course, fosters deeper understanding of the unique spiritual leadership capabilities that each spouse can bring to a marriage and family.

These complementary distinctions express themselves at the very core of marriage, leadership, and family life. Biologically, a woman's sexual identity is expressed more interiorly and receptively, while a man's sexual identity is conveyed more exteriorly and actively—forging a complementary sexual relationship. But the marital complementarity also extends beyond the physiological into other areas of family life and leadership. For example, as William E. May wrote in his essay, "Marriage and the Complementarity of Male and Female,"

> Both mothers and fathers must accept and nurture their children, challenge them and hold them to standards. But they do so in somewhat differing modalities, with the mothers accentuating acceptance and nurturance, the fathers challenging and disciplining.

May goes on to explain,

> This beautiful partnership, this wonderful covenant of love, unites human persons who differ in their sexuality and complement each other. Both husband and wife are to give and to receive; both are to image God. . . . But each is to do so in his and her indispensably complementary ways, the husband emphatically giving in a receiving

> sort of way . . . and the wife emphatically
> receiving in a giving sort of way.

In sum, men and women share equal dignity, but differ significantly in the way that God has designed them to fulfill their vocations within the family. Both the bodies and souls of spiritual heads and hearts complement one another. Man looks outward, while woman looks inward, and a family desperately needs both if they are to journey toward heaven together. The relationship is a fluid one, where men and women can share characteristics like self-sacrifice, generosity, and love; ultimately, though, their uniqueness is both essential and irreplaceable.

Leadership in Subjection?

Ephesians 5 is that New Testament reading that so many Catholic couples avoid when carefully selecting the Bible passages for their nuptial Mass, because, well, it tells wives that they should be subject to their husbands. Gasp!

I think it's worth revisiting these Scripture verses to see them in the light of the complementarity they actually encourage.

> Be subject to one another out of reverence for
> Christ. Wives, be subject to your husbands,
> as to the Lord. For the husband is the head
> of the wife as Christ is the head of the church,
> his body, and is himself its Savior. As the
> church is subject to Christ, so let wives also
> be subject in everything to their husbands.
> Husbands, love your wives, as Christ loved
> the church and gave himself up for her, that
> he might sanctify her, having cleansed her
> by the washing of water with the word, that

he might present the church to himself in splendor, without spot or wrinkle or any such thing, that she might be holy and without blemish. Even so husbands should love their wives as their own bodies. He who loves his wife loves himself. For no man ever hates his own flesh, but nourishes and cherishes it, as Christ does the church, because we are members of his body. "For this reason a man shall leave his father and mother and be joined to his wife, and the two shall become one flesh." This is a great mystery, and I mean in reference to Christ and the Church; however, let each one of you love his wife as himself, and let the wife see that she respects her husband. (5:21–33)

Let's focus specifically on some leadership principles that aspiring spiritual heads and spiritual hearts can take from these verses about the great mystery of marital love and leadership that St. Paul speaks of specifically in reference to Christ and the Church. Here is what I have learned from other families and how they practically apply this Scripture reading to their respective roles.

Spiritual heads . . .

- recognize that they are the head of their wives, the head of their families, leading with the authority given to them by Christ.
- know that this authority that comes from Christ also comes with great responsibility—namely, acting as Christ does for His Church, being willing to protect gallantly, lead boldly, and love sacrificially as a servant, even unto death.
- devote themselves to the work of sanctifying themselves

and their families, as Christ sanctifies the Church. They know that their job as the spiritual head of the household is to lead the way into heaven.

Spiritual hearts...

- recognize God's handiwork in his design for wives to be a "helper fit for" their husbands (Gen 2:18), seeing that they have the great privilege of encouraging (read: not nagging) their husbands to be the spiritual leaders God desires them to be.
- know that the respect they show for their husbands is reflective of the reverence they have for Christ, and that their supportive leadership roles as spiritual hearts motivates and strengthens their husbands in their spiritual headship.
- devote themselves to leading by example and love, not force, when their husband struggles in his own leadership. They know that their job as the spiritual heart of the household is to show love and to teach their families that love is the path into heaven.

Last year, I was enjoying a leisurely stroll around my in-laws' neighborhood with my then three-month-old son, RJ, when an unmarked white van began following us from street to street. I quickly made my way to my parents-in-law's house, seeking refuge behind a locked door and the sign on the front gate notifying solicitors and strangers that "My dog can make it to the fence in 2.3 seconds. . . . Can you?" That night I told Ray what happened, and before I could finish the story, he ventured online to purchase pepper spray. Two days later, an unusually large box arrived in the mail. When Ray got home from work, he excitedly opened the package to reveal the thoughtful gift he had purchased for me.

Out of the brown box came a giant can of pepper spray,

which bore a closer resemblance to a fire extinguisher than to the little perfume-sized defense mechanism I was expecting to see. Apparently, it would create a far-reaching pepper "fog" if diffused in the direction of a potential threat.

Unfortunately, what my husband was deadly serious about, I thought was a joke. As I chuckled, his heart sank, his hopes of guarding me to the Nth degree crushed under the heavy weight of my inappropriate laughter. All he wanted to do was protect me in the best way possible, and instead of being receptive, grateful, and sporting a new ready-to-conquer-evil-villains-in-the-neighborhood attitude, I was unsupportive and demotivating.

After I came around and sincerely apologized, that gigantic gunboat of pepper spray became one of my favorite gifts that I've ever received from him. It reminds me that my husband is here to guide, protect, and lead me, and that he needs my encouragement, gratitude, and love—not my derision, cynicism, and incredulousness. This mindset must extend in a special way to his spiritual headship and my supportive heartship.

Spiritual Leadership and the Bonding of Souls

When James and Susan Parkin first met, their spiritual lives looked totally different. Susan was the social butterfly of her Catholic young adult circle, frequenting retreats, leading parish ministries, and sporting an arsenal of Catholic books and CDs at home, in her car, and at work to learn from and to give to others. She loved her Catholic faith more than anything else in her life and couldn't wait to meet a man that felt the same way. Enter James, who, at the time they met, labeled himself as "spiritual, but rarely attends church."

"It was evident that James was the man," Susan reflected. "It just took trusting in God's plan for me and patience, which are both qualities that God obviously wanted to refine in me."

James hesitantly began attending Mass with Susan, and as their relationship evolved into marriage, James eventually felt God was calling him to enter into full communion with the Catholic Church.

"James' spiritual leadership over the past five years has evolved, from being open and intrigued to learning more about the faith, yet nervous about praying together, to leading us in a regular prayer," Susan explained. "James leads spiritually by his life. Often I find that I know more book details about the faith, but James—having no preconceived notions of the Catholic Church—encountered Christ with the beautiful purity of a child."

Over time, James, a husband, father, and senior network engineer, warmed up to the idea of being a spiritual leader, and now embraces his duties as the spiritual head of their family with intentionality. He demonstrates that spiritual growth takes time, and the more you work at it, the stronger you will become in your vocation to spiritual leadership.

"My whole life, I observed women as the 'churchy ones,'" James acknowledged. "The men seemed to miss church a lot or would not go. While dating and engaged to Susan, I became aware that the man is supposed to be the spiritual head. I now know that the responsibility to lead our family in faith is mine. I lead my family in prayer. I want my daughter to see her daddy going to Mass and know that is where God calls us to be." James mentioned being greatly influenced by the statistical evidence on the importance of fathers attending church for the effective faith formation of their children. "I want my family to be a holy family," James said.

He also recognizes obstacles to living out his call to lead and love his family toward heaven. James noted, "With the demands of daily work and life, it is easy to compartmentalize spiritual leadership as another 'job,' versus something that transcends all aspects of my day and life." Both James and Susan see their responsibilities as the spiritual head and spiritual heart of the household as a privilege and a challenge.

"Going from single to married is a bit of a shift when it comes to spirituality," Susan noticed. "Yielding to be the heart, when I am inclined to grab the reins as the head, takes work and humility. I find that if I'm doing a daily examination of conscience that I am more aware of ways that I fall short each day, so that the next time a similar situation comes around, I am more likely to respond differently." Letting James take the lead in certain situations allows their family to witness both a feminine and masculine example of faith in the home.

The Parkins learn from each other to become better spiritual leaders and help one another focus on the eternal importance of the often quiet, unseen work of spiritual leadership in family life. Susan elaborated, "James has taught me that it's often easier to go out of the home and lead spiritually than it is to truly live out the faith in family life. God calls us to our domestic church first, and the grace of the Sacrament of Matrimony has bonded our souls, so that each of our actions truly affects the other."

Portrait of a Spiritual Head

Statistical and anecdotal evidence demonstrates that parents are the number one influence on the faith lives of young people. As James discovered on his journey into the Catholic faith, study after study finds that the role of the father in particular is critical in handing on an active spiritual life to his children. Without a strong spiritual head to guide them, children can so easily be lost to a culture that deprives them of the meaning, purpose, and hope for living that only Jesus Christ can provide, in and through His Church.

So what exactly does a strong spiritual head look like? What do certain husbands and fathers do, what traits do they possess, and what habits do they master that help to make them standouts in modeling for their family a faith worth imitating? Here are some of the unique qualities strong spiritual husbands and fathers model for their families in a special, masculine way:

An attitude of surrender. Strong spiritual heads are willing to hand over control to God, recognizing that He is the one who is Lord of their lives, their families—everything. They recognize that it is a sign of true masculinity, not weakness, to call on God for guidance and to surrender to His will.

Humility. While our culture spends time touting pride as a masculine virtue, strong spiritual heads are modeling the virtue of humility for their families, making daily steps to conquer their desire to always be right, or to seek acclaim and accomplishment, instead opting to devote time to showing their families how to give credit and glory to God, seeking to please Him above all else.

Boldness. Strong spiritual heads are bold about their Catholic faith—at home, at work, and in public. They aren't afraid to make decisions in light of their faith and to let others know and see that they are Catholic, not just in name, but in active practice.

Openness to fellowship. While the prevailing norm is to think about sharing meaningful conversations about life, faith, and family as a feminine activity, strong spiritual heads recognize that they shouldn't try to go it on their own when it comes to spiritual leadership. They acknowledge the importance of seeking accountability, encouragement, and fraternity with other men and make it a regular habit to do so.

Friendship with St. Joseph. Strong spiritual heads cultivate surprisingly beautiful devotions to Our Blessed Mother, but they also lean on the intercession of St. Joseph to help them in their immense task of caring for their family's physical, emotional, and spiritual needs, as St. Joseph gallantly did for Mary and Jesus.

Portrait of a Spiritual Heart

There's no arguing about how important a spiritual head's faith is to the family's relationship with our Lord and the Catholic Church He founded. But what about the spiritual heart? Countless Catholic lay men and women, priests and religious point to their mother's faith as an anchor in their own spiritual journey. Perhaps you have your own memories of your mother clenching her rosary beads at her bedside before she started the day's work, or the prayers that she taught you when you were still young enough to sit on her lap during Sunday Mass or nighttime prayer.

My own mother's expert living of her vocation as a spiritual heart has made her the most remarkable role model in my life. I've noticed in her and in many other strong spiritual hearts some uniquely feminine aspects of spiritual leadership:

A habit of sacrifice. Strong spiritual hearts seize frequent opportunities to give of themselves, to die to their own desires, inclinations, or preferences for the good of others, especially for the good of their husbands and children. They master the art of self-gift, giving everything from their bodies to their time, talent, and energy for those they love, and they find joy in doing so.

Quiet trust. Over time and through prayer, strong spiritual hearts inch their way toward an almost unshakable trust in God and in His will for their lives, especially within their families. They offer their children to God, recognizing that they are first and foremost *His* children, and then they throw themselves into His divine mercy, trusting He will care for them and for their families.

Reliance on grace. Strong spiritual hearts rely on God's grace to tackle the colossal responsibility of motherhood. His grace animates their daily lives—carrying them through their household chores and their efforts to provide emotionally, physically, and spiritually for their families—and comforts them when they feel exhausted and worn. They see His grace at work in their family life, and they can't imagine living without it.

Unseen strength. Utilizing the particular gifts, talents, experience, and energy God has given them, spiritual hearts are pillars of physical, emotional, and spiritual strength, serving and loving the Lord and their families with all their *might* (Dt 6:5). While their spiritual heads display masculine strength for others to see, the strength of the spiritual hearts often goes unseen, but its presence is most certainly felt and needed by their families.

Friendship with Mary. Strong spiritual hearts take their leadership cues first and foremost from Our Blessed Mother, the immaculate model of spiritual heartship. Seeing her as the most exemplary wife and mother that ever walked the earth, they implore her intercession and cultivate an intimate relationship with her to help them become more beautifully virtuous like she was and is. They ask her to wrap the mantle of her love and protection around each precious member of their families.

What are some traits that both strong spiritual heads and spiritual hearts have in common? Many of them possess a sense of humor and lightheartedness about the craziness of family life, seeing it as an adventure where mistakes will inevitably be made. They also share a profound awareness of their lack of qualification for the lofty task of guiding their families toward holiness, recognizing that they could not do it on their own apart from God's grace.

Spiritual Heads and Hearts Fulfill Unique, Complementary Roles

The Catechism explains,

> Physical, moral, and spiritual difference and complementarity are oriented toward the goods of marriage and the flourishing of family life. The harmony of the couple and of society depends in part on the way in which the complementarity, needs, and mutual support between the sexes are lived out. (2333)

Fulfilling your unique and complementary roles as a team of spiritual leaders, each with unique gifts to bring to your family, holds the key to unlocking purpose, organization, peace, and joy in your home and in the world in which you live. It's just that important.

Head to Head

"Being the spiritual head of the family is a difficult challenge that has been modeled for us by Jesus Christ. Jesus was sacrificial and loving; He cared for His flock and loved it to the point of death. You, as a father and husband, have a responsibility, on a daily basis, to do things in your life to better know your Catholic faith and to live it more fully. As a husband, what are you doing to get yourself to heaven? What are you doing to get your wife to heaven? Together, with your wife, what are you doing to get your children to heaven? This can happen if we are making daily, incremental steps to grow in our faith."

—*Greg Willits,*
media guru, radio host, podcaster, and author

Heart to Heart

"Becoming a mother has really helped me understand my role as the spiritual heart of my family. Men and women are uniquely gifted, and each of our impact on family life is designed to be unique as well. My previous experience in the working world definitely required more head than heart. Most of my mothering experience seems to require more heart than head . . . and stretches me to love beyond what I thought I was capable of. If you're struggling with the spiritual roles in your marriage, find the right priest to meet with. Nurturing the challenging areas in your marriage is so important; it's better to reveal your weakness than to appear like a 'perfect Catholic family' on the outside while letting your marriage slowly break down behind closed doors. As Mother Teresa said, 'Love begins by taking care of the closest ones—the ones at home.'"

—*Susan Parkin,*
wife and mother

Your Leadership Action Steps

Beginner

Review the characteristics of spiritual heads and hearts discussed under the headings "Portrait of a Spiritual Head" and "Portrait of a Spiritual Heart." Choose one characteristic that you think you could improve upon, and reflect on that characteristic this week or month and try to incorporate the practice of it into your daily life. (Example: As a spiritual heart, if you struggle with Quiet Trust, make a resolution to pray, "Jesus, I trust in You," when stress comes creeping in.)

Intermediate

Sit down with your spouse and discuss how you are living

out your unique and complementary roles as the spiritual head and spiritual heart of your family. What do you believe are your own greatest strengths and weaknesses in this role? What do you believe are your spouse's greatest strengths and weaknesses in his/her role? Choose one characteristic discussed under the headings "Portrait of a Spiritual Head" and "Portrait of a Spiritual Heart" that you think you could improve upon, and reflect on that characteristic this week or month and try to incorporate the practice of it into your daily life. (Example: As a spiritual head, if you struggle with Openness to Fellowship, make a resolution to join a men's group or find a faith-filled accountability partner to encourage you in your effort to become a stronger spiritual leader.)

Advanced

Pray and reflect on the above verses from Ephesians 5 on a daily or weekly basis for the next month, reflecting on how effectively you are living out this Scripture passage in your own family. Calling on the Blessed Mother and St. Joseph's intercession, ask the Holy Spirit to guide you toward one characteristic discussed under the headings "Portrait of a Spiritual Head" and "Portrait of a Spiritual Heart" that you think you could improve upon, and reflect on that characteristic this week or month and try to incorporate the practice of it into your daily life. (See *Beginner* and *Intermediate* steps above for examples.) You can also choose a different characteristic to work on that comes through discussion with God in prayer or through conversation with your spouse.

2

They Have a Mission

*"Each family finds within itself a summons
that cannot be ignored and that specifies
both its dignity and its responsibility:
Family, become what you are."*
–Pope St. John Paul II, Familiaris Consortio, no. 17

Toward Intentionality

Patrick Lencioni, husband, father, *New York Times* bestselling author, and founder and CEO of a management consulting firm in the San Francisco Bay Area, has written numerous business books, selling millions of copies around the globe. Among his impressive titles there is a book that is unlike the others. In *The Three Big Questions for a Frantic Family*, Pat applies his leadership and management techniques specifically to family life. The content of the book is practical and applicable, and the ideas innovative. Yet this refreshing book doesn't sell nearly as many copies as his business books do.

"People are willing to invest time and energy into running their business," Pat explained. "But when it comes to their family, they think, 'Oh, I don't need to do that.'" Pat offers an interesting explanation for this lax attitude toward family management. "I think the reason why is because of this wonderful thing called *unconditional love*. They think, 'My family isn't going to fire me, but my boss might.' That's a very bad way of looking at it."

Over the years, Pat has noticed that organizations that fail to clarify a vision for their future devolve into what he calls "the generic," or unintentional. "The family is the most important organization in our lives," Pat argued. "Why do we spend so much time at work planning, clarifying what success looks like and how we're going to get there, and then we come home and we're so reactive and unintentional about family life? It doesn't make any sense."

Years ago, Pat and his wife Laura, a stay-at-home mother to their four sons, decided to apply some of the business tools that he was using with Fortune 500 companies at home, and it worked. What the Lencionis discovered—and expertly teach others—is something that every family must come to terms with if they desire to live a life of effective spiritual leadership: a family needs a mission to guide it toward intentional living.

A Culture of Mission-less Families

Successful businesses and Fortune 500 companies today generally have well-defined, intentional missions. Pat Lencioni has made a career of helping businesses become more focused, organized, and strategic in executing their missions. So what about our families? Why do we allow our families—the most important organizations in our lives—to wander through time without a clear purpose, without specific objectives or strategies, without a defined, agreed upon, unifying mission as a team, to guide us for the foreseeable future toward success, toward intentionality? Today we live in a culture of mission-less families, and many of these mission-less families are experiencing a depressing fate. For decades, we have been watching marriages crumble. Still many more families are surviving but not thriving, giving in to the chaos that we have come to expect family life to be.

Why do we as a culture, as executives of our family organizations, and as individuals desiring to be strong spiritual leaders for our family, settle for less in our family life than we would accept in our professional lives?

The Thomas family is one family choosing to live counter-culturally, witnessing that every family has a purpose, one that makes them invaluable to society as a whole. "David and I realize that a family is not merely a collection of individuals," explained Theresa, mother of nine, ranging from ages twenty-seven to ten. "A family is a unit itself—a community. A family is also a microcosm of society. All of society's problems can be traced to the family. To use a biology metaphor, a healthy cell contributes toward healthy tissue, which makes a healthy organ, which makes a healthy system, a healthy body. The same can be said about the family. A healthy family positively impacts a community, which impacts a city, a state, a nation, the world. Strong families make strong cultures. Likewise, weak or failed families negatively impact culture."

David, a husband, father and attorney, and Theresa, a stay-at-home mother and Catholic author, have ensured that their family's mission helps nurture each family member individually, while also emphasizing the importance of their serving one another as a community. Their family's mantra, "It is a privilege to serve," helps guide their interactions with each other and positively influences the larger community around them. They refuse to be a mission-less family in our culture, and more families making that same decision mean that we, as a Church, can slowly but surely reverse our culture of drifting families.

The Mission of the Largest Family You Know

In the Gospels, we find clear, mission-oriented statements that Christ offers for the largest family you know, His Catholic Church:

> Go therefore and make disciples of all nations, baptizing them in the name of the Father and of the Son and of the Holy Spirit, teaching them to observe all that I have commanded you. (Mt 28:19–20)

> And he said to them, "Go into all the world and preach the gospel to the whole creation." (Mk 16:15)

The Church is called to go and make disciples, to teach and to preach the Gospel. So *evangelization*—the proclamation of the Gospel, the announcement of the good news that Jesus Christ was raised from the dead—is critical to the life and vitality of the Church. In other words, evangelization is the Church's mission.

Pope Paul VI, in his apostolic exhortation *Evangelii Nuntiandi*, clearly stated:

> Evangelizing is in fact the grace and vocation proper to the Church, *her deepest identity. She exists in order to evangelize*, that is to say, in order to preach and teach, to be the channel of the gift of grace, to reconcile sinners with God, and to perpetuate Christ's sacrifice in the Mass, which is the memorial of His death and glorious resurrection. (no. 14, emphasis added)

Could we say that the mission of the Catholic Church—the family of believers—which is evangelization, is also the mission of the domestic church, the church of the home? Absolutely. We—the family, the domestic church—"exist in order to evangelize," to build up the kingdom of God. Evangelization is part of our "deepest identity."

The Mission of Each Catholic Family

Our Catholic faith makes it clear that evangelization is both the mission of the largest family you know—the Catholic Church—and the mission of smaller Catholic family units, the domestic churches made up of individuals like you and me, our spouses, and our children. It makes sense that the mission of Catholic families must support and take part in the mission of the Church as a whole. So, simply put, the mission of Catholic families is to share good news.

Catholic families do this in two ways.

First, internally: Catholic families share good news *within* their families. This means proclaiming and building up the kingdom of God in one's own home, helping each family member achieve salvation in Jesus Christ. Your family does this by living as a "community of life and love," as Pope St. John Paul II describes in his apostolic exhortation *Familiaris Consortio*, helping each family member find fulfillment through union with God in heaven someday.

Second, externally: Catholic families share good news with the world. This means being a living *witness* of communal life and love with everyone a family encounters. By demonstrating your belief in the God-given worth of every member of the family and making a radical self-gift to each of them, those outside of your home see an authentic reflection of God's image and likeness in your family unit. This helps lead more souls to believe in the Gospel message and build up the kingdom of God. Perhaps this is why the

Church considers family the vital cell of society, and, as Pope St. John Paul II phrased it in his *Message for the XXVII Day of Peace*, why "the family contains in itself the very future of society."

In the same paragraph of *Familiaris Consortio*, Pope St. John Paul II offers a powerful directive: "Each family finds within itself a summons that cannot be ignored and that specifies both its dignity and its responsibility: Family, become what you are" (17). Family, become what you are and you will find purpose and meaning in your family life. Family, become what you are and help lead one another to sanctity. Family, become what you are and you will have a dramatic and positive impact on the joy and holiness of the families around you. Family, become what you are. Fulfill your mission.

Seeking Sanctity First

At the time Javier and Kayla Sanmiguel's worlds collided, they each had a strong sense of what they wanted out of life. "When Javier and I met, we both had guiding principles for our lives," Kayla described. "At various phases of my life I had fallen in love with different thoughts, including Leon Bloy's quote, 'The only great tragedy in life is not to become a saint.' Javier, a born leader, wanted every day and every experience to count for something. Because we felt individually driven to become more fully ourselves, and because our view of marriage was that of 'two becoming one,' the creation of a joint mission came naturally. As we began having children, we translated the mission of our marriage into a family mission."

The Sanmiguels adopted an informal, verbal mission until the birth of their first child. Then they recognized the importance of having a tangible guiding purpose to share with their kids. "The creation of our mission was relatively simple; we wrote down everything we wanted for our family and found that every goal sprung from the desire to love Christ and each other and become His saints in a way characterized by faith, joy and trust—so that is what we wrote!" Kayla remembered.

Javier and Kayla already see how it focuses and motivates them and their family. "Our family mission statement has already immensely benefitted our family," Kayla acknowledged. "Case in point: Last year, I was a miserable pregnant lady in the midst of a particularly miserable pregnancy. I was inclined to be grouchy, whiney, and lazy. On many occasions, recalling our mission helped me hold back a bitter comment, whine internally instead of to my husband, or comfort my son although it required that I get out of bed. I still have quite a bit of room to grow, but I am encouraged by the small victories."

Javier admitted that family missions are not always easy to live out. Like business missions, it takes hard work to make them a reality. "There will always be failure. That shouldn't scare us," Javier explained. "Falling short helps us grow and acknowledge what we need to work on." As with most things in life, it is not the fact that you have fallen, but how you choose to recover from the fall that matters.

"If we want healthy families, we first need to define what a healthy family looks like," Kayla reflected. "Without a vision—a clear goal for ourselves and for our families—we are unable to measure growth or know how to achieve it. A family mission statement explains why our family exists and what we hope to accomplish, and don't we want all of our family members to be on the same page when it comes to that?"

Los Sanmiguel Family Mission:

To be a boldly Catholic family, seeking **sanctity** before all else, with visible **faith**, contagious **joy**, and genuine **trust** in Jesus Christ.

Your Mission: The Foundation on Which Leadership is Built

Even if you consider yourself advanced in every characteristic of strong spiritual leadership, if you do not have a mission you run the risk of drifting off course when friction presents itself in family life. The spiritual leaders I interviewed that you will meet throughout this book know where they are going, they know what they want out of family life, and they make sure their families are on board, too.

As we have already discovered, generally speaking, your family's mission is to share the good news. But now it is time to get specific. The benefits of creating a unique mission are many. It has the power to unify, focus, and guide your family to achieve your goals and work for one another's good. Having a family mission statement can literally transform your family life.

Identify Your Mission: A Practical How-To

First, a few things to keep in mind before starting:

• Know that the process is just as important as the product. Designing a family mission isn't always a smooth ride, but you will learn a lot about your family as you go. Cherish that opportunity. Embrace the bonding, the meaningful conversations, and the honesty that you will experience as a family during this exercise.

• Make it a special event. Call a family meeting. Order the family's favorite takeout or cook a favorite family meal to kick off the experience. You can even pick a special place to host your mission designing process. The goal is to create an atmosphere of excitement and to make memories.

- Give everyone an opportunity to speak and ensure that everyone listens.
- Do not give yourself time constraints. You may need to schedule a sequel to your mission-storming night, and that's okay.

Your step-by-step guide:

Pray before you begin. Ask the Holy Spirit to guide you through the process so your family can come up with a mission that ultimately brings glory to God. Come up with your own spontaneous prayer, or use this one:

> Lord, thank you for bringing us together as a family to discern our mission. Help us to articulate how we can serve You by sharing the good news in our family and with others. Bless our conversation and open our hearts to Your will for our family life. We ask this through the intercession of our Blessed Mother Mary and with the intercession of the saints who are dear to our family in particular (list them here). And, as always, we ask all this in the name of the Father, and of the Son, and of the Holy Spirit. Amen.

Elect a scribe. (It may help if you pre-elect one to avoid any conflict.)

Ask questions, and have the scribe take note of family members' answers. Some good questions to ask include:

- What kind of family do we want to be?
- What virtues or characteristics do we want to be known for? (Examples: patience, honesty, justice, joy, hospitality, sacrifice)

- What one, two, or three words would you use to describe our family?
- What do we need to do to best act like Jesus to one another in our family?
- What families inspire us and why?
- What are our top three priorities in family life?
- What unique gifts do you have that you can offer the family?
- How do we think our family is called to serve our Church?
- How can we as a family better serve our community and society as a whole?
- What are our most cherished, core values? (Examples: faith, discipline, creativity, adventure)

Use your creative leadership capabilities to think of more questions as the meeting unfolds. If your children have questions, let them pose some, too.

If you have some very introverted children, you may want to consider taking some quiet time to reflect on some of the questions and write them down silently as individuals before sharing aloud.

Review the notes taken by the scribe and come up with three to ten main ideas (remember, sometimes less is more). These are the ideas, characteristics, values, virtues, or goals most often repeated or agreed upon by the family as a whole. You can even cast votes to determine the main ideas. Have the scribe list them on a separate sheet of paper.

Write your family mission. Missions are extremely unique to each family. I have read ones that take the form of multiple paragraphs. I have seen families come up with a numbered or bulleted list of statements or phrases. Other families have a single, concise sentence, preferring brevity for the sake of memorization.

Anand and Lindsey Bheemarasetti devised a brief but beautiful mission statement to remind them to focus on what matters most in life. As Anand described, "If we have reminders for paying bills, getting groceries, wishing people happy birthday, and to exercise, we should also have reminders to grow in holiness and character."

The Bheemarasetti Family Mission:
To **seek Christ** by listening, respecting, and supporting each other at home, and to **serve Christ** by giving hope through prayer, tithing, and corporal works of mercy as a family in the community.

Still others go with a list format, like the Lencionis, who list their core values, followed by their family strategies and then their single most important immediate priority (which usually changes every three months, and can be a spiritual, physical, or financial goal).

The Lencioni Family Values and Strategies:
Our core values are
- forgiveness
- creativity
- standing up for what's right even when it's unpopular

Our family strategies are
- to be maximally involved in each other's lives
- to make faith the center of everything we do

This exercise is all about customization for *your* family.

Another consideration may be to write the mission from your notes as a couple, representing your family as the spiritual leaders, and then present it to the rest of the family for agreement. Again, you will know what is likely to work best for your family.

Sign it. Some families like to have special signing ceremonies to celebrate the occasion and signify agreement by all family members. You could sign the actual mission statement, the back of the paper, or another special sheet designated for signatures (which works well if you intend to have a plaque or canvas made of your family mission statement, rather than a framed piece of paper).

Pray after you finish. Offer a prayer of thanksgiving to God, asking Him to guide your family on a daily basis to accomplish your mission and achieve your outlined goals.

Frame your mission or have it made into a plaque, canvas, fridge poster or magnet, or some other form of presentation, and display it in a prominent place in your home.

Refer to it. Incorporate your family mission into family prayers. Refer to it when making decisions as a family, and teach your children how to refer to it when making personal choices. Seize teachable moments using your mission as a motivator and helpful reminder of your family's desired way of acting, living, and goal-seeking.

Revise as needed. As your children age and your family grows and changes, you may feel like adjusting your mission. I would not recommend making changes to it a habit, but be open to amending it if you feel like it would better reflect your family's purpose at some later date.

Spiritual Heads and Hearts Have a Mission

In his pastoral letter, *Family: Become What You Are*, Archbishop Samuel Aquila noted:

> The family is called to greatness! But today there is much confusion about the nature and purpose of marriage, which is the foundation of every family. Why are people experiencing this confusion? Many intermediate causes

can be cited, but the root problem is that married couples and families are not living according to their created purpose and are not embracing the fulfilling but challenging truths revealed to us by Christ through His Church.

Now that you have developed a defined mission that will help you achieve the goal of growing in your "community of life and love" and help you live according to your created purpose, your role in exercising spiritual leadership in your family becomes clearer and more vital. Husband and father: As the head of the family, how are you going to help lead the family to realize its purpose? Wife and mother: As the heart of the family, how are you going to help inspire the family to stay true to its mission?

Finally, if you want more time to reflect on your family mission, or if you want further examples from other couples of the way that they express their faith within their family lives, feel free to continue reading the subsequent chapters and come back to this chapter later—or even at the end of the book—as a way to synthesize what you have learned and experienced, and establish a vision that will guide you forward.

Head to Head

"Make sure that everyone in your family, and everyone who knows your family, understands what you're about. When you are faced with decisions to make, instead of looking around and asking, 'What is everyone else doing?' ask yourself, 'What is our family about and how does it mesh with our plan?' Don't be reactive. Be intentional."

—Patrick Lencioni,
husband and father, founder and CEO of The Table Group
and co-founder of The Amazing Parish

Heart to Heart

"There is a reason parenthood is considered an awesome responsibility; we are charged not only with the physical health and wellbeing of our munchkins, but with the growth of their character and their development into the persons the world needs them to be. This call demands that we seek unceasingly to live out our family mission, to get up after every fall, and to do this in sight of our husbands and children."

—Kayla Sanmiguel,
stay-at-home wife and mother

Your Leadership Action Steps

Beginner
Display the phrase, "We are a community of life and love" in a visible place in your home, letting this serve as a mission statement for your family. Try to refer to it often and evaluate how your family is reflecting the "community of life and love" that you are called to be.

Intermediate and Advanced
Complete the *Identify Your Mission: A Practical How-To* activity above.

3

They Have Strong Marriages

"If a marriage is to preserve its initial
charm and beauty, both husband and wife
should try to renew their love day after day,
and that is done through sacrifice,
with smiles and also with ingenuity."
—St. Josemaria Escriva

A Union That Glorifies God

My husband and I, starry-eyed fiancés at the time, sat next to one another at the expansive wooden conference table at my home parish, awaiting our good friend and priest who was going to celebrate our nuptial Mass, Fr. Henry, to return with the results of our pre-marital inventory. Ray was chuckling at my obsession with getting a super-compatible score, himself totally unmoved by the quiz-taking process. Fr. Henry sauntered into the room, teasing about how miserably we failed the inventory—which both he and Ray kept reminding me you can't fail—before discussing our answers together. Apparently, Raymond and I were on the same page about pretty much everything—faith, in-laws, finances, communication, habits . . . *phew*. I sat back and let the relief sink in. Just as I thought: we were perfect for each other.

But right when I was enjoying that head-in-the-clouds

feeling I had gotten accustomed to throughout our engagement thus far, Fr. Henry's mood shifted from cheerful to serious.

"You guys, I have to be honest with you," he said, his normally jovial demeanor taking on a distinct somber tone. "The devil is going to attack you. He is going to attack you hard. Because the devil loves to attack marriages, and he especially attacks strong marriages, because strong marriages glorify God."

We nodded in understanding, but we didn't really understand the weight of his comment until we had been married a few months, and then a few years. Those of you reading this after decades of marriage probably understand his remarks to an even greater experiential extent. The devil despises a loving, faith-filled marriage. Consequently, he will seize every opportunity to weaken or destroy it, but his master plan to attack marriage has been going on for a very long time.

In the Beginning . . .

In the beginning, God created Adam and Eve, the original match made in heaven. Adam and Eve really were perfect *and* perfect for each other. Their holy union, mirrored after God's own Trinitarian union, must have irked Satan beyond imagination. He could not allow their relationship to grow and blossom unharmed by his interference. So he mettled, and the result was devastating, not only to Adam and Eve individually, but to Adam and Eve as a couple. As the Catechism states, "As a break with God, the first sin had for its first consequence the rupture of the original communion between man and woman" (1607). Satan inserted a chasm of sin between Adam and Eve, and between the once perfect couple and God. He must have felt like he succeeded in wrecking their union, but that's not actually true.

Indeed, the devil hasn't ceased in his efforts to attack marriage throughout the course of salvation history, and perhaps in what appears to be a magnified way into our present day. But we can fight back. Every marriage that chooses love over pride, sacrifice over selfishness, the glorification of God over a life of sin, wins spiritual battles against Satan for their marriage. On a smaller scale, even little, daily actions *for* marital intimacy and *against* marital strife damage demonic attempts to stain the beautiful plan that God has for marriage, helping all of us married persons become stronger spiritual leaders and glorify God through marriages that grow in holiness and love, one simple act or choice at a time. It's through those daily small acts and choices to have a strong marriage, in a culture that continues to weaken this sacred relationship, that couples are transformed into the strong spiritual leaders that God created them to be.

Your Choice: What Kind of Marriage Do You Want to Have?

"Jim and I decided before we were married, both individually and collectively, that divorce was never going to be an option," remarked Meg Beckman, Jim's wife, mother of five, and Catholic school counselor. "This is a scary choice, a choice that involves an incredible amount of trust—trust in God, trust in the other person, and trust in oneself. However, it has become one of the pillars of our marriage and an access point of God's grace."

Meg believes that every couple has a choice. They can be a part of the statistic of marriages that end in divorce, or they can choose to prioritize, to nurture, and to protect their marriage—with God's help—every day of their lives.

"Leadership is always built on a foundation, and in the family that foundation is the marriage itself," expressed Jim, husband, father, Catholic graduate school lecturer and founder of the YDisciple youth ministry program. "It takes three to get married though—husband, wife, and God. We have found that faith is such a critical aspect of our relationship, that with it missing from the equation, we would probably topple over no matter how great things might seem between us. If my priority isn't my marriage, then there is also no foundation for our kids to rest upon. To me, this is the foundation of spiritual leadership."

But nurturing the marital foundation of family and spiritual leadership isn't an easy thing to do, especially when the threats against marriage are blatant and forceful. "The media, secularism, and post-modern philosophies have all uniquely converged to threaten the very fabric of marriage," Jim noticed. "Think about it for a moment from Satan's perspective: if you wanted to weaken the faith and humanity of an entire culture, where would you focus your attack? The family." Conversely, Jim and Meg have realized, "If we want to succeed in our marriages, we have to focus energy and attention on it. Our efforts have to be intentional, consistent, and vigilant."

For the Beckmans, their efforts are realized in a variety of ways. Prayer is central in their personal lives, marriage, and family, and time spent together as a couple is an intentional habit. They also implemented the wise counsel of a priest, who advised them early on in their marriage, as Meg explained, "to form a small group of other strong, Catholic couples that gather a few times a month to share our ups and downs, pray with and for one another, and to receive advice. This, too, is what sustained and strengthened us when our personal prayer was dry and circumstances were almost too much to bear."

Another major factor in strengthening their relationship over their twenty-year marriage has been their openness to life and God's plan for growing their family, which Meg described, involves more than keeping her womb open to life, but also each of their hearts, minds, and souls open to life. "Physical barriers between couples can result in spiritual barriers to God's grace and even natural expressions of love. Conversely, through the 'free flow' of grace and love that our hearts have experienced through Natural Family Planning, Jim has grown in God's love for him and in his ability to express his love and affection for me, while I have gained confidence in my femininity and ability to nurture and love our children." Both Jim and Meg have seen their spiritual leadership flourish as a result, recognizing that the benefits of their total receptivity of one another and God's will for their lives have spilled over onto their children.

"The fruit of this has been a security our children have in us, and then in themselves," Meg noted. "Our oldest son was saying how he sees so many of his friends struggling with insecurity about who they are. I asked him what he thought about that. After a few moments, he said that he thought most of these friends came from families whose parents struggled in their relationship with each other. He said, 'I mean, you and Dad aren't perfect, but I know your love for God and each other is what keeps you close and together. This makes me feel secure and humbly confident in myself.' Our son's words made us grateful for each other and all the work that the Lord has done in our hearts and marriage."

In his masterful work on marriage, *Three to Get Married*, Archbishop Fulton Sheen writes:

> In all human love it must be realized that every man promises a woman, and every woman promises a man that which only God alone can give, namely, perfect happiness. [Many couples] fail to realize that human feelings tire and the enthusiasm of the honeymoon is not the same as the more solid happiness of enduring human love.

Perhaps the greatest choice that the Beckmans have made for their marriage has been the choice to pursue that kind of enduring human love. "I always have to remind myself that love is a decision, not a feeling," Jim elucidated. "I have to make choices all the time in my marriage for love, even when I don't feel like it, even when it is not convenient." Spiritual leaders like Jim and Meg do not waste too much emotional or physical energy grasping at fleeting feelings of bliss; they instead actively pursue God-like love because, no matter how hard they have to work, they know it's worth it.

A Strong Marriage: The Foundation of Family Spiritual Leadership

Marriage is a foundation stone for spiritual leadership—*the* foundation stone for spiritual leadership in the family. A couple with a strong marriage has the greatest chance of forming the best spiritual environment in their home. What makes for a strong marriage? The most refreshing, yet unsurprising thing that I learned about the marriages of strong spiritual leaders is that they are exceptional at forming certain habits that many marriages in our culture today do not practice. Some of these habits include:

Praying with and for one another. Couples with strong marriages recognize that prayer is one of the most intimate experiences they can share and that prayer nourishes their physical, emotional, and spiritual lives as individuals and as a couple, drawing them closer to God and one another.

Being unreservedly open to life and having a holy, ful-filling sexual life. They know that God's plan for sex in marriage leads to the greatest marital satisfaction. Since sex is God's design, it makes sense that couples find the most happiness when they live within His plan for it.

Working through minor or intense marital strife. Strong spiritual leaders with strong marriages take their nuptial vows seriously. They put in the hard work necessary and ride out the bumps and bruises that marriage sometimes causes along the way, since they know that their marriage is meant to last until death do them part.

Believing and acting on the belief that they are meant to serve one another. Marriage is an institution that embodies the connection between love and service. Couples with strong marriages believe that one of the aims of marriage is to be a servant to the other.

Forgiving well and often. Despite how unbelievably hard it can be, strong spiritual leaders refine their apologizing and forgiving skills, and frequently take advantage of the Sacrament of Reconciliation to become better at forgiving and asking for forgiveness.

Couples with strong marriages also spend time and energy nurturing certain marital behaviors that are still almost universally accepted as important tools, yet some do not make the effort to become experts at utilizing them. Strong spiritual leaders acknowledge that their marriage can't thrive without these marriage-building behaviors:

Practicing effective communication. Couples with strong marriages are exceptional at communicating with one another. They learn the skills to effectively articulate their feelings, needs, struggles, goals, fears, and dreams, and then they act upon what they communicate to improve their marriage.

Growing in affection. Besides little, important acts of affection (hand holding, kisses and hugs, love notes, and the like), couples with strong marriages make a concerted effort to have time to reconnect by planned dates where they regularly take time to grow in their affection for and attraction to one another as lovers and friends.

Expressing gratitude. Simply put, they say thank you in word and action . . . a lot. Strong spiritual leaders know that they are appreciated in their marriage, because their spouse is always reminding them of it.

Being joyful toward each other. These couples enjoy the simple gifts and blessings of everyday life, especially within their own marriage and family—a fruit of the joy, humor, and stability that characterize their marriage.

Fostering teamwork. Couples with strong marriages let their family see them working together as a leadership team. This can be as easy as asking their spouse regularly, "What can I do to help you? Is there something I can do to make your day easier today? How can we work together to accomplish this duty?"

Handling conflict constructively. They let their arguments work *for good* for them. Strong spiritual leaders take the opportunity to learn and grow from conflict. They turn their conflicts into opportunities to make their marriage stronger—something that isn't easy to do, but as with the other habits, it is what makes them standouts in spiritual leadership.

Strong spiritual leaders recognize that marriage is about both love and sacrifice. Our culture today often emphasizes the love aspect, but grossly underemphasizes the sacrifice part. It is through sacrifices both big and small—which sometimes require legitimate suffering—that love blossoms into something stronger, more beautiful, godlike, and lasting.

In Pope St. John Paul II's Apostolic Exhortation *Familiaris Consortio*, he notes, "The sacrament of marriage is the specific source and original means of sanctification for Christian married couples and families" (no. 56). Becoming a saint is *never* easy. Sanctity requires the daily decision to die to oneself in order to live more fully for God and others. "It is by following Christ, renouncing themselves, and taking up their crosses that spouses will be able to 'receive' the original meaning of marriage and live it with the help of Christ (cf. Mt 19:11)" (CCC 1615). Somewhat ironically, this kind of death to self and taking up of one's cross brings inexplicable happiness. Marriage is the means of our sanctification—the vehicle that steers families toward heaven and authentic, eternal joy.

I Will Love You and Honor You, All the Days of My Life

Mike and Laurie Carlton lead an astonishingly successful marriage ministry at their home parish. Most nights, more than two hundred people are in attendance, hungry for strategies and information to help their marriages thrive and their faith grow. If you asked the Carltons just ten short years ago if they anticipated that they would be leading a thriving marriage group and helping couples grow and restore their marriages, they would have thought you were crazy. Ten years ago, Mike and Laurie were on the brink of separating.

In 2004, thirteen years into their marriage and despite Mike's conversion to Catholicism from Presbyterianism two years prior, the Carltons felt like they had grown apart. Mike was traveling every week for work, while Laurie was busy at home taking care of their boys.

"We had a marriage crisis. With four children all under five years old, our marriage almost fell apart," Laurie described. "By the grace of God, it was saved. With our gift of free will, we could have destroyed all of the beauty in it, but fortunately, it was built on solid, holy ground," Laurie recognized. "We realized that all of the terrible advice we heard from various people—'kick him out,' or 'kids are flexible and can deal with divorce just fine,'—was all garbage. It became obvious to Mike and me that marriage is fragile, and how, without our Catholic faith, it probably would not have mended. We realize now not only how fortunate we are, but also that most marriages can be saved, too."

This realization that most marriages *can* be saved and, better yet, can thrive, stirred Mike and Laurie to action. "Six months after almost moving out, we renewed our vows," Mike explained. "We realized that Catholic couples experience marriage preparation programs prior to their wedding, but receive very little support for their actual marriage along the way. Often, when couples have children, they get used to being Daddy and Mommy and forget about being husband and wife. This was partially our story and we see it repeated often." So, after overcoming their own marital crisis, the Carltons started a ministry called Marriages are Covenants (MAC) at their home parish to help couples foster stronger marital relationships and encourage couples to renew their vows often as a reminder of their commitment to one another and to God. Their ministry work continues to strengthen their own marriage, too, making them better spiritual leaders for their family. "When our marriage is doing well, the whole family benefits," Mike has noticed.

Now, Mike, husband, father, and global vice president of an orthopedic biologics company, and Laurie, wife and stay-at-home mother of six, focus on important marriage builders—prayer, communication, and affection, to name a few—to continue to nurture their marriage and strengthen them as spiritual leaders for each other and for their children.

Laurie discussed, "On a daily basis I pray for Mike: for his interaction with colleagues at work, for safe driving in the car or on a flight, for our relationship, for his choices regarding parenting, for his strength as the holy leader of our family. I also pray that I love him despite little irritations and that I follow him along the path that God has chosen for him." The Carltons also take time to communicate more often with each other, even in small ways. "I touch base with Laurie sometime during the workday, and I try to leave notes for her before I leave for work, with a simple 'I love you,'"

Mike mentioned. Finally, affection plays a more prominent role in their marriage now, as a constant, tangible reminder of their love—not just for them, but for their kids, too. "When Mike and I embrace in front of them, they love it. Every time I hug Mike, I think of the advice a dear friend gave me: 'Look over your husband's shoulder each time you embrace, thank God for the gift He gave you—this big strong man who loves you.' So I do."

When presiding over the wedding of twenty couples in St. Peter's Basilica in September of 2014, Pope Francis encouraged the married couples to rely on Christ's redemptive sacrifice to help strengthen their marriages in moments of weakness, discouragement, and woundedness. "The love of Christ, which has blessed and sanctified the union of husband and wife, [is] able to sustain their love and to renew it when, humanly speaking, it becomes lost, wounded or worn out," Pope Francis described. The Carltons experienced this love of Christ firsthand, and relied on it to heal and uplift their marriage.

Conflict is How Leaders are Made

Leaders are made or broken in times of conflict. Conflict doesn't have to be destructive; it can actually be positively transformative. Couples who learn to negotiate well have maximal potential to become great spiritual leaders.

All organizations, good stories, and human relationships have naturally occurring conflict. Leaders are, by nature, passionate people, so it makes sense that their passion would overflow into their arguments as well. Sometimes, when all that passion is let loose and goes untamed, what could have been a rational—even somewhat heated—conversation turns into a tornado-like force ripping through a couple's closeness and seemingly destroying all possibility of healthy resolution. The challenge becomes using that passion, discipline, and creativity that leaders are known for and channeling it into constructive negotiation, and then forgiving and asking forgiveness—often and well—when needed.

I loved the raw wisdom that Jim Beckman shared with me about conflict in their marriage. First, he reminded me of the words in Sirach 2.

> My son, if you come forward to serve the Lord, remain in justice and in fear, and prepare yourself for trials. Set your heart right and be steadfast . . . and do not be hasty in time of calamity. . . . Cling to him and do not depart. . . . Accept whatever is brought upon you . . . in changes that humble you be patient. For gold and silver are tested in the fire, and acceptable men in the furnace of humiliation. (1–5)

Jim aptly noted, "This passage flies in the face of modern thinking, which would have us believe that when we decide to follow God, everything is going to go right—even and especially in marriage, right? But these verses tell us just the opposite. The choice to follow God is to choose the path of purification, and that comes through suffering. Marriage and family life is literally filled with opportunities for that. Obviously, there are joys and innumerable blessings, but those are far more enjoyable because of the hard work engaged along the way to get to them."

Jim recounted a story about how he and Meg once powerfully changed the way they handled conflict by identifying the root cause of most their arguments. Essentially, Jim felt most undermined when his honor was called into question or disrespected, while Meg experienced the most hurt when she felt unappreciated or unloved. Over time, and with the help of a spiritual director, the Beckmans learned how to short-circuit their arguments. "I would tell Meg how valuable she was to me and Meg would tell me that, as far as she was concerned, I couldn't fail, and that she loved me, inadequacies and all. Now I'm not saying that we never argue or even fight anymore—that would sure be nice! But the intensity has definitely diminished. More importantly, we had a new self-awareness about the driving force underneath almost every conflict that ever happened." Beginning to look at things from one another's perspective helped bring about positive change.

Jim highlighted this important lesson: "The bottom line is to focus on each other instead of the conflict. The conflicts are just the stuff of life that we have to navigate through. But our spouse? That's who we're on the journey with. And learning to love that person, flaws and all, is what is going to get us to heaven. The conflicts actually give us the challenges we need to continually grow in that capacity."

Conflict also gives people the opportunity to practice genuine apologies and forgiveness. The ability to ask for forgiveness well is an art. I still regularly fight the urge to prompt a moment of apology and forgiveness like this: "I'm sorry your feelings were hurt, but you misunderstood what I said." Leaders instead say something like, "I'm sorry (without qualification). I ask for your forgiveness for speaking uncharitably to you"—or for whatever the offense is. Leaders genuinely apologize, *asking* for forgiveness for the real wrongs they have done, and do so without qualification.

Furthermore, true leaders forgive. They don't hold grudges and they believe in Jesus's words in Matthew 6: "For if you forgive men their trespasses, your heavenly Father also will forgive you; but if you do not forgive men their trespasses, neither will your Father forgive your trespasses" (14–15). In time, the strongest spiritual leaders forgive, not out of obligation or desire to be forgiven by the heavenly Father, but out of pure sorrow for inflicting hurt and out of love for the other and for God.

Spiritual Heads and Hearts Have Strong Marriages

In 2012, on the commemoration of the married saint, Bridget of Sweden, Pope Benedict XVI called Christian married couples to become "the sweet and smiling face of the Church," inviting them to live out the call to be "the best and most convincing messengers of the beauty of a love supported and nourished by the faith, a gift of God which is given to everyone abundantly and generously, so that day after day they can discover the meaning of their lives."

Would you consider yourself and your spouse to be examples of "the best and most convincing messengers of the beauty of a love supported and nourished by the faith"? Would others look at your marriage and see "the sweet and smiling face of the Church"? It's important to remember that the end of marriage is less concerned with becoming perfectly happy (because only God can make us perfectly happy) and more concerned with becoming better people. Strong spiritual leaders are committed to becoming, and helping their spouses become, saints.

Head to Head

"I have found that when I am engaging in a relationship with God, He takes me to amazing places. He challenges me, stretches me, and opens up my heart in ways I had never imagined. Flowing out of that relationship, my capacity to love my wife seems to be expanded in ways I had never thought possible. The opposite is true as well. In times when I start allowing busyness and distractions to keep me from prayer and pursuing my relationship with God, I start sliding back into my old self—selfish, occupied, distant, irritable. Husbands and fathers, we are about no earthly task here! We are building the kingdom in our family, one living stone at a time! Marriage is about me laying down my life for my wife and for our children. That's not something that comes naturally to anyone. The beauty of it all, though, is that the Lord's invitation is not just for me to lay down my life, but for me to lay down my 'struggle' to lay down my life. And He will walk with me every step of the way if I let Him."

—Jim Beckman,
husband and father, graduate school lecturer

Heart to Heart

"Both Jim and I agree that the greatest challenge to marriage is ourselves. The key to success in marriage is receptivity . . . being receptive to him, who he is, and what he has to offer. Do whatever it takes to make your marriage all that God intended it to be! Never give up. I can remember the pain and sadness I was in when Jim and I were struggling in our marriage. I thought, 'Is this ever going to end?' Well, it did, and it can for you, too. Just keep being receptive to the Lord's love and be grateful for all of God's gifts, and He will lead you to healing and freedom."

—Meg Beckman,
wife and mother, school counselor

Your Leadership Action Steps

Beginner

Go online or to your local Catholic bookstore and read about the life of a married saint.

Intermediate

Prayer, communication, and affection are important marriage builders that you can engage in every day. Every day for the next week, incorporate at least one heartfelt prayer for your spouse into your daily routine, one special form of communication (a love note in a lunchbox or on a bathroom mirror, an email list of things you love about your spouse, an evening where you dream together about the future), and at least one playful or romantic act of affection (for example, I like to surprise my husband by running down the hall like a little kid and throwing my arms around him into a big squeeze hug). Once you have done this for a week, try to continue doing these things on a daily basis, being creative and heartfelt with your prayer, communication, and affection each day.

Advanced

Reread the bulleted lists of countercultural habits and marriage building behaviors under the heading "A Strong Marriage: The Foundation of Family Spiritual Leadership." Discuss with your spouse which of these habits and behaviors you are good at exhibiting, and which need the most improvement. Choose one that needs improving, and come up with a plan to make progress in that behavior or habit this month. (For example, if you struggle with forgiving well and often, commit to working on making more sincere and unqualified apologies and to saying, "I forgive you," rather than "That's okay" after your spouse asks for forgiveness.) To encourage one another, verbally or in writing, acknowledge those times when your spouse does a particularly good job acting on that behavior or habit.

4

They Prioritize Prayer

*"Because I cannot depend on
my own strength, I rely on Him
twenty-four hours a day. . . .
My secret is very simple: I pray."*
—Blessed Mother Teresa of Calcutta

The Genius of St. Teresa's Prayer Philosophy

St. Teresa of Avila offers a simple and powerful prayer philosophy: *If you don't pray sometimes, you can't pray always.*

When it comes to our prayer lives, most of us probably fall somewhere in the middle—somewhere between praying sometimes and praying always. The prayer warriors I admire most are not prayer experts, but they are remarkable in their conscious effort not to settle for a stagnant prayer life. I recently heard a priest describe how most fifty-year-olds have the same prayer life that they had as eight-year-olds. I want something more than that, for God, for myself, and for my family.

Over the years, I noticed the importance of seizing many "sometimes" moments to pray, in an effort to work toward the grand task of trying to live my whole life as a prayer to God. Growing up, I was somewhat atypically fortunate to have parents who were powerful prayer models, leading my sisters and me in prayer before my dad left for work and we rushed to the bus stop. It was not unusual to hear my dad say to an acquaintance over the phone, "Let's end in prayer," and to hear him ask the gentleman sitting next to him on an airplane, "Can I pray for you right now?" My mom was a regular visitor to the adoration chapel as our family's powerful intercessor. Her prayer life—characterized by a beautiful humility and quiet strength—stirred such wonder in me, as it truly occupied the central place in her life. She taught me to take small glances at the crucifix in our home throughout the day, pray for a stranger in need when the loud blares of a siren passed by, offer sufferings for a friend or family member battling illness, and to give thanks for my many blessings. Most importantly, perhaps, my parents taught me how to talk to Jesus spontaneously and genuinely, as my friend, father, teacher, and God, along with modeling for me how to pray using the Bible and by accessing the arsenal of prayers given to us through the Church.

Even if you had a totally different upbringing in prayer—or no exposure to prayer at all in your home growing up—you can be the one that infuses prayer into your family life *now*. If you aren't doing it already, start praying sometimes, and then gradually work your way toward praying always.

Portrait of a Praying Heart: Prayer as a Battle

Praying sometimes or *anytime* is often a struggle. If you feel like your prayer life is a battle, you aren't alone. Even strong spiritual leaders struggle with being dedicated to prayer.

"Prayer is a battle. A battle that is sometimes lost, sometimes won. But make no mistake; it is a battle," described Michelle Wright, a wife, mom, and teacher. "The only reason I feel comfortable giving advice on this topic is because I know just how important it is to keep fighting and how discouraging it can be when we feel like we are losing," Michelle admitted. "The most important thing I can say about prayer and family life is this: just keep fighting the battle."

Michelle opened up about the challenges that family life can pose to an active prayer life. "I have come to realize that there are different seasons to prayer and each season has its own beauty and its own challenges," Michelle reflected. "Rather than thinking about my prayer life as a straight line with a beginning and an ending, I have come to see it as a spiral going deeper and deeper into the mystery of God. The seasons come and go with time, and eventually I find myself again in a familiar place. The question I have to ask myself then is not how many spiritual books I have read, how many novenas I've prayed, or even how many hours I've been able to spend in adoration, but rather, 'How much more am I able to love in this given situation than I was the last time I was here?' and 'Am I able to find God in this particular setting in a new and more meaningful way?'"

Recalling some of her past seasons of prayer, Michelle noted the difference between prayer in her youth and prayer in her family life, which appears less glamorous, and is often marked by frustration and discouragement. So Michelle exercises creativity in her prayer life as a wife, mom, and spiritual leader. "I started to look at my day and think of all the things that filled it. No two days looked the same; however, there were common activities that took place on a regular basis. Doing the dishes, folding the laundry, driving to the store, and even brushing my teeth became regular opportunities for prayer. I realized, in part through the promptings of some wise girlfriends, that I could easily assign a specific type of prayer to each one of those chores. When I do the dishes, I count my blessings. While I am folding laundry, I start thinking of all of the other people who asked me to pray for them, and I intercede on their behalf and offer that chore as a prayer. Brushing my teeth at the beginning of the day and at the end of the day, I spend two minutes offering up my own petitions. I am far from being perfect in my execution of this concept, but these small changes have definitely made a difference in my prayer life."

The Wrights take small and meaningful steps to make prayer a part of their family routine, too. "Beside Sunday Mass, we always pray before meals, even if we are in public. We say a Hail Mary every time we hear a siren. I am constantly saying the spontaneous, quick prayers: 'Help me out Lord,' 'Lord, give me patience,' and lots of 'Praise the Lord!' I want my son to know that I am constantly thinking about the Lord and talking to Him even if it is not a formal setting. We are also in the routine of praying as a family every night before bed." In these ways, they continue to "fight the prayer battle," winning victories that draw them closer to God each time they pray together.

A Family that Prays Together . . . Is a Family Led by Strong Spiritual Leaders

Why do strong spiritual leaders make prayer such an important habit in their lives? The *Youth Catechism of the Catholic Church* (YOUCAT) describes prayer as "the great gate leading into faith" (469). Strong spiritual leaders know that it is their responsibility, privilege, and joy to knock on the door and enter through that great gate and to lead their families through it, too. The effort and the battle to pray is part of what makes us Christians striving to draw closer to Jesus and become more like Him through conversation with Him in prayer.

I've found that strong spiritual leaders know a few other important things about dedication to prayer:

It's soul food. They know that nourishing their spiritual life through prayer is even more important than nourishing their physical life through food. Since their soul is eternal, they know how important it is to feed it well through prayer.

It's about quality time and fostering a relationship. Strong spiritual leaders know that if they want a deeper relationship with Jesus, they have to do what anyone desiring a deeper relationship with someone does: spend time with each other. And with God, that is done through prayer. In prayer we reach out to God, not as some distant being, but as a Father and Friend, who is right there with us as we pray.

They can't live without it. Like Blessed Mother Teresa noted, "Because I cannot rely on myself, I rely on Him, twenty-four hours a day." Strong spiritual leaders dedicated to prayer know that they *need* God to help them lead as spiritual heads and hearts, and to be happy, holy, and at peace.

Jesus said so. Jesus commanded us to pray. Strong spiritual leaders see His command throughout Scripture and obey His word:

- Watch and pray that you may not enter into temptation. (Mt 26:41)

- Have no anxiety about anything, but in everything by prayer and supplication with thanksgiving let your requests be made known to God. (Phil 4:6)

- Continue steadfastly in prayer, being watchful in it with thanksgiving. (Col 4:2)

- Pray constantly. (1 Thess 5:17)

The spirituality of the family hinges on it. Strong spiritual leaders know that their prayer influences the spiritual lives of the entire family. They know that their prayers with and for their family have tangible effects on each of their family members and that their example of prayer sets the model for their spouses and children to follow.

It doesn't have to be perfect to be efficacious. These words from the Catechism ring in the hearts of strong spiritual leaders: "*Humility* is the foundation of prayer. Only when we humbly acknowledge that 'we do not know how to pray as we ought,' (Rom 8:26) are we ready to receive freely the gift of prayer" (2559, emphasis added). With humility as the cornerstone, they realize that prayer, a gift, doesn't have to be offered perfectly to be valuable. Fumbled words and feeble hearts are accepted graciously by an unconditionally loving Father.

It requires patience. Strong spiritual leaders remind themselves that they can't become perfectly holy overnight, nor will their prayer lives always be what or where they want them to be. But they keep praying and trying to grow in prayerfulness anyway.

Jesus and Mary are great role models of prayer. In prayer, we respond to God's love with the gift of ourselves. No one has done this more perfectly than Christ, who conformed His human will perfectly to the divine will through constant prayer. Our Blessed Mother also modeled for spiritual leaders what it means to give of oneself in prayer. Through her fiat she gave God permission to work in and through her in powerful ways.

Strong spiritual leaders know that prayer opens the door to God's outpouring of love in their lives. Prayer glues individuals to God and binds couples and families together, so strong spiritual leaders make it a top priority to pray—individually, as a couple, and as a family.

The Church's Arsenal of Prayers

Being Catholic means that we are never at a loss for what to pray or how to pray, and strong spiritual leaders are particularly good at taking advantage of the guidance and prayers offered by Jesus and His Church to enrich their spiritual lives.

Prayer can be both public (the Mass) and private (meditation in your bedroom), vocal and silent, formal and informal, and as its own type of communication, it takes on different forms: adoration (worship), contrition (acknowledging sinfulness and expressing sorrow for our failings), acts of charity (expressions of love), petition (asking God for things we need), intercession (asking God for things others need), and thanksgiving (expressing gratitude for our blessings).

One of the most fascinating things about prayer is that it is unique to every person. Mary Voss, wife, mother of five, and small business owner, actively pursues focusing in prayer by kneeling, "a good discipline which helps me overcome struggles with distraction," she described. She and her husband of twenty-three years, Dr. Paul Voss, a professor of Shakespeare and seventeenth-century literature, imbed some of the Church's beautiful prayers into their regular routines and everyday family life. "We include prayers before all meals, prayer on the way to school in the morning, prayer at the sound of every siren, prayers at night and frequently in the midst of bickering, stress, challenge, tears, or joy. I say short prayers all day long at the office about direction and wisdom. As our kids become older and more independent, we want them to habitually turn to prayer in time of need or gratitude. My husband and I wanted talking to God, or asking the Blessed Mother for guidance, or calling on a patron saint for intercession, to be a natural response throughout the day," Mary elaborated. "We also believe in the power of the Rosary and in the Divine Mercy Chaplet. The beauty of formal prayer is that even when I am unfocused, I often complete my prayers with a changed heart or with peace."

You don't have to become experts at a certain method of prayer or feel pressure to be exceedingly eloquent, especially when praying out loud with your spouse or family. Spiritual leaders have a different mindset: no methods are needed (though structured prayer, as Mary pointed out, is both beautiful and helpful) and no wordsmithing is required. They talk to God like they talk to their father or friend, as someone who loves to hear from His beloved children. God desires a totally one-of-a-kind relationship with each of us, with our marriages, and with our own unrepeatable families in prayer.

In the Gospel of Luke, one of His disciples asked Jesus, "Lord, teach us to pray" (11:1). Perhaps these words comprise the first prayer that you as a couple, desiring to be strong spiritual leaders, turn to right now. Ask the Lord to teach you to pray, and to allow the Holy Spirit to help guide you to the family prayer life He wants for you.

Wondering where to start in personal or family prayer? See the appendix for a quick, go-to list of some of the many favorite prayers and prayer traditions that aspiring spiritual leaders use in their personal and family prayer lives, and with each other.

Whatever prayers you decide to pray in your own life or with your family, remember that the act of praying itself—rather than what you pray or how you pray—is the greatest offering and the hardest part of the battle. We live in a Martha culture, where we often use the excuse that we are too busy to pray. The most important thing you can do *right now* is to pray. Remind yourself of that simple fact throughout the day and then just do it.

Portrait of a Praying Head: Entering into Vulnerability

"Prayer requires humility and vulnerability. In turning to prayer, we implicitly acknowledge our own inadequacy and dependency on something greater than ourselves," recognized Matthew Warner, husband, father of four and founder and CEO of Flocknote. "When we are able to turn to prayer in the company of our family, it opens up those relationships not only to the graces of prayer, but to the healing that comes from genuine humility. Continually entering into this vulnerability, this truthfulness, together creates bonds that will survive the toughest trials of life."

Matt knows that his family's prayer life can thrive only when his personal prayer is strong. "If I want to be able to give something to my wife and kids, then I have to receive it first. It really is that simple. And the concept applies to spirituality as much as anything else," he noticed. "I remember a moment after we had our first child—and many similar moments since—when it hit me that I'm responsible for this precious little soul. That reality drives you to your knees, turning to the One who can do all things. If I don't fill myself up spiritually, I will not be able to fulfill my purpose of giving my family what they need."

To nurture his own spiritual life, Matt tries to focus on prayer as an end in itself. "The days that end well usually start well—with prayer. The days I 'don't have time' to pray are the days that seem to be the most stressful. They are spent trying to do all the wrong things. Ultimately, I find that a minute of prayer saves me hours of toil and that all those tasks I busy myself with are nowhere near as important as the praying itself. In other words, prayer is not just a means to an end (i.e. the secret to a better, more focused, successful day), but it is the end in itself. It is the fulfillment of my day."

But let's be practical—it's not always easy to pray, as a family or as an individual. Matt regularly experiences what it is like to tackle the ups and downs of family and personal prayer. His advice? "Just do it. It doesn't have to be poetic or articulate, and it doesn't have to take very long. Just pray something and let it grow from there. Many days my 'morning prayer' consists of making the Sign of the Cross when I wake up. It's not as much as I'd like, but it's something.

With children this is even more applicable. Even if all you do is pray a Glory Be with your child before bed each night, you're doing infinitely more than no prayer at all. Keep it simple when you start. Having simple, easy prayers that you pray as a family each day at specified times is an easy way to ground your family in prayer and begin the building of important habits that will shape you and your children for the rest of your lives. Then keep striving to improve. Our kids are all fairly young still, so another thing that works great for us is praying in song. Singing the Our Father is something they get excited to participate in and it's become a part of our daily routine. It also ties in nicely to their participation in the Mass (since we sing it the same way at our parish on Sundays). But, still, sometimes crying babies or stubborn toddlers will make it difficult."

For Matt and his wife Lauren, entering into the vulnerability that prayer calls for is an important exercise for their family. "Making the effort counts for something. It's rarely perfect execution, but even if you're all distracted or it's cut short, prayer still works. It's like exercise, it's still good for you even if you don't feel like doing it. And often it's especially those times that you feel like it's not working that God is working most on you."

The Fundamental First (and Last) Minutes

Archbishop Fulton Sheen once aptly pointed out: "There are two ways of waking up in the morning. One is to say, 'Good morning, God,' and the other is to say, 'Good God, morning!'" Which way do you wake up in the morning?

Most of us wouldn't dream of starting the day without so much as a thought about someone we love. Yet so many of us begin our heavily-scheduled days without so much as a thought directed toward Jesus, the one whom we should love above all else. St. Gemma Galgani offered a simple thought to Jesus in her fundamental first minutes: "Can you see that as soon as the day breaks I think of you? . . . I love you, Jesus!" Maybe that's your fundamental first-minutes prayer: "I love you, Jesus." Maybe it's a repetition of Fulton Sheen's cheerful greeting, "Good morning, God." Maybe you prefer to start the day by praying over the daily Mass readings or by reading other passages in Scripture. If you aren't using your fundamental first minutes for prayer, try it. Pick a prayer that works for you and see what happens. You may quickly notice that your other prayer rituals and routines throughout the rest of the day all seem to depend on and draw energy from your prayer in those fundamental first minutes.

It didn't surprise me to learn that the strong spiritual leaders I have learned from and admire start and end their days with prayer. One woman I spoke to admitted that as parents, many of us aren't good at taking time for ourselves, arguing that our family responsibilities outweigh our need to recharge with some personal quiet time. But that car ride to run an errand by yourself may be your only time *alone* with the Lord that day. Those moments before the children wake up may be your *only time alone* with your heavenly Father in a hard-working twenty-four-hour time span. If you, like me, wake up to a toddler poking at your eye and are thrust into your day without sufficient time for prayer, speak to God whatever few but meaningful words you can, and then plan a time to dialogue with Him before bed. Even Jesus believed in making prayer the first activity of the day: "And in the morning, *a great while before day*, he rose and went out to a lonely place, and there he prayed" (Mk 1:35, emphasis added). If Jesus did it, that's a good enough reason for me.

A Spiritual Sign of Love

When I was interviewing individuals and couples for this book, I was eager to learn about their prayer lives. Dedica-

tion to prayer is a necessity for spiritual leadership. Many of
the couples I interviewed have been married for many years
and have anywhere between one and a dozen children. John-
Paul and Annie Deddens, on the other hand, were celebrating two years of marriage at the time I interviewed them for
this chapter. Despite their rather new entry into marriage
and family life, I was inspired by their dedicated prayer lives
individually and as a couple. Their example serves as a reminder that you don't have to be a certain age, have celebrated a silver anniversary, or even have any kids in the home
to pursue strong spiritual leadership. The Deddens have
inspired thousands of other individuals, couples, and families of all ages, shapes, and sizes to grow in their dedication
to prayer, too, through their impactful ministry called *Pray
More Novenas.*

"While we were dating, Annie asked me to pray a novena
with her," John-Paul recalled. "Because of my past lack of
discipline, resulting in a failure to pray all nine days of the
novena, and the subsequent guilt, I turned her down. Later,
I realized that my inconsistent prayer life was not a good
excuse to not try again. I realized that, like many others, I
am constantly checking my email and I have trouble sticking
to novenas. So, I decided to start PrayMoreNovenas.com to
help others where I needed help." Today, more than 130,000
people from around the world join John-Paul and Annie in
praying novenas year-round, thanks to their novena reminder email service.

Recognizing how prayer strengthens their spiritual leadership, Annie and John-Paul make a daily effort to put prayer
at the center of their lives and marriage and their relationships with God and each other.

"Christ is the model leader and servant. If I am to lead,
serve, and love my wife like Christ leads, serves, and loves
His Church, I need to be constantly growing closer to Him.

Prayer is the primary means by which any of us can grow closer to God," John-Paul pointed out.

Annie not only turns to certain prayers for strength, comfort, and spiritual growth, but also to certain prayer role models. "There are some saints that I'm particularly drawn close to who have helped me shape my prayer life though reading and learning more about them and their prayers. St. Anne and St. Joachim experienced infertility for a long time in their marriage before they had their daughter, Mary. So I look to St. Anne when I may get tired of praying for something that has yet to happen. Then there's St. Thérèse who experienced a debilitating illness but placed all of her trust in God. I look to her for strength and greater trust when I'm going through something rough. And then there's our Mother, Mary, my greatest prayer role model. I can imagine her doing so many things for St. Joseph that I do for my husband, and I think of not only *what* she may have done, but also *how* she did those things. I think of her attitude, her tone, and her will to serve, and I try to emulate that."

Annie also noted the tangible effect that prayer has on their marriage on an ongoing basis. "When we're praying together daily, that's when I feel more joyful, more at peace, and more in love with my husband and our life together," Annie elaborated. "On the other hand, when we've gone a while without praying the Rosary together or intentionally discussing our trust in God regarding what concerns us most, that's when I feel discontent and I see myself trying to fill that void with something other than God. That's also when I may become less generous and less charitable towards John-Paul."

Beside praying *in* their marriage, the Deddens believe in the importance of praying *for* their marriage. "If we do not pray for each other, we are missing a big part of marriage," John-Paul explained. "Praying for your spouse is the best sign of spiritual love for him or her. If she's sick, I pray for her healing. If she's worried, I pray for calm. If she's sad, I pray for joy. But, I also pray that I will be able to love her better and more fully." Annie prays for John-Paul in return. "I pray that he will be a good leader for our family. I pray that he will be able to overcome any obstacles to holiness. I pray that he will grow closer to God so that we may live as He wills us to. I also pray that I will be a greater wife for him and a greater helper for him. I think it's essential that I recognize my role in his journey to heaven. I take it very seriously, so I pray that we will both lead each other towards what is good, what is right, what is true."

Spiritual Heads and Hearts are Dedicated to Prayer

It was no surprise to me that almost every single spiritual head or spiritual heart I interviewed for this book spoke about dedication to prayer—individually, as couples, as a family—even if I didn't yet ask them about it. The Youth Catechism of the Catholic Church (YOUCAT) asks, "Is it enough to pray when you feel like praying?" The response is this: "No. Someone who prays only when he feels like it does not take God seriously and will leave off praying. Prayer thrives on faithfulness" (490; cf. CCC 2652). Even strong spiritual leaders struggle with prayer, but they know that their prayer life and their family's spiritual well-being requires their faithfulness in giving it their all.

Head to Head

"It's especially important for husbands to realize the unique responsibility they have as spiritual head of the family. For the most important things, the buck has to stop somewhere if we want to make sure responsibilities get done. I think a good marriage assigns responsibilities similarly. When it comes to making sure your family is a family of prayer, the buck stops with the man. If my family doesn't pray, it's my fault. I must be the spiritual leader. And I know that starts with the daily habit of personal prayer."

—Matthew Warner,
husband and father, founder of Flocknote.com
and TheRadicalLife.org

Heart to Heart

"I know how important prayer is. I know I need it. Why is it so darn difficult to pray as a wife and mother? Because it is so important! I want to give my son that same formation my parents gave me, to know the joy and the peace of Christ. I also know I need prayer if I want to be the wife, mother, and woman that God created me to be. I often have to remember, though, that different seasons of life require a new approach to prayer. A very wise and patient priest once told me, 'You need to learn how to pray as you can, not as you can't.'"

—Michelle Wright,
wife and mother, teacher

Your Leadership Action Steps

Beginner

Pick one of the prayers listed in the appendix. Incorporate it into your personal or family prayer life. Praying it at roughly the same time each day—for example, in the morning before breakfast or right after family dinner—will help ensure it becomes a regular part of your routine. You can even set a reminder on your phone or put a sticky note on the fridge, your bathroom mirror, or nightstand to help ensure that you pray! Keep in mind that if you aren't taking advantage of praying in those fundamental first minutes of the day, this would be a great time to add that chosen prayer.

Intermediate

On a piece of paper, phone, tablet, or wherever you like to make notes, write out some of the activities you do every day that could be good occasions for certain types of prayer. Examples of recurring activities may be: showering, driving to or from work, taking a walk, doing laundry. You probably would be surprised at how many repeated habits you have. Like Michelle in the "Prayer as a Battle" section above, match a few of those daily routines with a type of prayer you could offer during that time. (Some of the different forms of prayer mentioned above were contrition, acts of charity, petition, intercession, thanksgiving, and adoration.)

Advanced

Schedule time once a week or at least once a month to spend time alone with Jesus in Eucharistic Adoration. If it's not offered in your parish at a time you can attend, go sit in a quiet chapel or sanctuary and take time to reconnect and just *be* with the Lord.

5

They Make the Home a School of Virtue and Culture

"The only true riches are those that make us rich in virtue."
—Pope St. Gregory the Great

Education in the Virtues: A Lost Art of Leadership

Our modern education system typically emphasizes values rather than virtues. Education in virtue, a virtue being "an habitual and firm disposition to do the good," is becoming a lost art of leadership (CCC 1803).

There is a difference between value and virtue. A virtue is a disposition to *do* the good, not just to *know* the good or to value it. Most people value fidelity in marriage, yet some, despite their values, are unfaithful to their spouse. Virtue helps you not to just know that fidelity is good, but to be faithful. Ordinary men and women become saints not by merely knowing that they should love God, but by loving Him, not just by valuing humility, but by being humble.

The Second Vatican Council's declaration on Christian education, *Gravissimum educationis*, is abundantly clear about the role of parents in educating their children: "Since parents have conferred life on their children, they have a most solemn obligation to educate their offspring. Hence, parents must be acknowledged as the first and foremost educators of their children. Their role as educators is so decisive that scarcely anything can compensate for their failure in it. . . . Hence, the family is the first school of those social virtues which every society needs" (no. 3).

As spiritual leaders, education in the virtues is critical to this faith and life formation in our families. Moreover, we are called to turn our homes into schools of virtue, where ordinary men and women discover the virtues they need to be transformed into extraordinary saints. Most of us learned at some point in our childhood that friends rub off on each other. When we become a closer friend of Jesus, He rubs off on us. We grow in humility, like Christ is humble, in courage, like our courageous Savior, in love, like our God who is love. His perfect model of virtue becomes our gain, and the training we get from the school of friendship with Our Lord carries over into the school of virtue we build in our homes. In other words, becoming a leader in virtue begins with fostering a deep, committed relationship with Jesus Christ.

Virtue: The Stuff Leaders Are Made Of

Michelangelo finished sculpting his masterpiece, the Pietá, at the ripe young age of twenty-four. As the story goes, when the work was unveiled to the public, the young Italian sculptor planted himself in the crowd of admirers, bending his ear to hear what people thought about his first great work in the city of Rome. As you might expect, the crowds loved it (as they still do), and were in awe of the sculpture's grandeur and the skill of its anonymous artist. Nobody believed the youthful, relatively unknown Michelangelo when he told them he was its maker. Their disbelief ate at Michelangelo, who, one night, crept into the basilica and engraved his name on the sash across the chest of the Blessed Mother. Understandably, Michelangelo was later regretful for his prideful action, which now was visible to everyone, stamped right across the woman who is the paragon of humility!

Today's culture leads us to believe that wealth, fame, and *pride* is the stuff leaders are made of. But this couldn't be farther from the truth. True leaders excel in virtue, first and foremost leading with the virtue of humility, the virtue that Michelangelo was lacking that night in the darkness of the basilica with his chisel in hand. It is tempting to desire acknowledgement for the often hidden work we do in our homes, but living virtuously behind closed doors is a gift to your family and a glory to God—and that alone is enough. Virtues lay a foundation of power, strength, and ability. Virtues are the building blocks of character, the foundation stones of strong spiritual leadership.

You don't need to etch your name to the work you do as a spiritual leader in your family life, because your life of virtue or vice will serve as an obvious signature.

A School of Cardinal Virtues: Acquired by Human Effort

Real virtuous living is not just about doing the good, but about doing it promptly, consistently, easily and joyfully. This makes practicing virtue even more challenging, but with the aid of God's grace, deep transformation can occur. "With God's help, they [human virtues] forge character. . . . The virtuous man is happy to practice them" (CCC 1810).

There are a number of virtues that strong spiritual leaders emphasize as part of their schooling in virtue. Let's briefly focus on seven of them: four cardinal (moral, human) virtues and the three theological virtues.

The Cardinal Virtues

"*Prudence* is the virtue that disposes practical reason to discern our true good in every circumstance and to choose the right means of achieving it" (CCC 1806). Prudence helps direct both our passions (on the inside) and our actions (on the outside). Through seeking counsel, making judgments, and being decisive, strong spiritual leaders who practice prudence "live their lives on target," Catholic author Dr. Edward Sri describes.

"*Justice* is the moral virtue that consists in the constant and firm will to give their due to God and neighbor" (CCC 1807). Justice is not so much about what is owed to us, but rather, it gives spiritual leaders the keen eyes and decisive action to respect the rights of others. Through religion, we give God His due, making practicing our Christian religion an act of justice, and not something we do just for our personal gain or satisfaction.

"*Fortitude* is the moral virtue that ensures firmness in difficulties and constancy in the pursuit of the good" (CCC 1808). Fortitude allows spiritual heads and hearts to transform into magnanimous, patient, persevering leaders. Those who possess fortitude are able to overcome obstacles, conquer fear, and sacrifice themselves for others.

"*Temperance* is the moral virtue that moderates the attraction of pleasures and provides balance in the use of created goods" (CCC 1809). Romans 13:14 states, "But put on the Lord Jesus Christ, and make no provision for the flesh, to gratify its desires." When our insensibility tempts us to say yes to what isn't good for us, temperance helps the spiritual leader say no. Ultimately, though, temperance is about saying yes to the freedom that comes from restraining our appetites, so that we can live godly lives unhindered by an enslavement to sin and earthly pleasure.

A School of Theological Virtues: The Greatest of These is Love

The Catechism has this to say about these next three virtues, which leaders must possess to be truly *spiritual*: "The theological virtues relate directly to God. They dispose Christians to live in a relationship with the Holy Trinity. . . . The theological virtues are the foundation of Christian moral activity; they animate it and give it its special character. They inform and give life to all the moral virtues. . . . There are three theological virtues: faith, hope, and charity (cf. 1 Cor 13:13)" (1812–1813).

The Theological Virtues

"*Faith* is the theological virtue by which we believe in God and believe all that he has said and revealed to us, and that Holy Church proposes for our belief, because he is truth itself" (CCC 1814). St. Augustine once wrote that "faith opens the door to understanding; unbelief closes it." Faith involves belief, trust, and reliance. It's not a feeling, but something much deeper. It is an act of the intellect, prompted by the will, and it allows us to do one of the most important things we can do as spiritual leaders: say yes to God.

"*Hope* is the theological virtue by which we desire the kingdom of heaven and eternal life as our happiness, placing our trust in Christ's promises and relying not on our own strength, but on the help of the grace of the Holy Spirit" (CCC 1817). Catholic philosopher Dr. Peter Kreeft says this about hope: "Hope is like headlights. It is not easy to drive without headlights in the dark." The theological virtue of hope gives life to our soul and energy to our spiritual leadership; it brings the expectation of positive outcomes in the hard work we put into family life. Hope is our response to God's promises, which He always fulfills.

"*Charity* is the theological virtue by which we love God

above all things for his own sake, and our neighbor as ourselves for the love of God" (CCC 1822). God is love, and our
vocation, our greatest duty in life, is to love. The theological
virtue of love is the greatest of all the virtues. It is the very
essence of God. The quality that makes spiritual leaders and
saints beautiful is their love. St. John of the Cross emphasizes the importance of this virtue: "At the end of our life, we
shall all be judged by charity."

When strong spiritual leaders make an intentional effort
to grow in and practice the cardinal virtues and to accept the
beautiful gifts of God in the theological virtues, they experience more disciplined, freeing, purposeful, and joy-filled
lives. Though it requires effort, the hard work is worth the
results, which shine through in their families.

Seeking Ordinary Opportunities and Moments of Growth

"For us, the key to a virtuous family life is not a planned
structure in which we inculcate virtues," explained Brandon
Vogt, husband and father of four. "We don't sit down and say,
'Today, kids, we're going to work on temperance!' Instead,
we seek opportunities in the ordinary ebbs and flows of daily
family life to teach. It might be when our son cries because
he desperately wants to go to the park but we aren't leaving
for another two hours—that's a chance to discuss patience. It
may be when our daughter wants to be the first child to leap
into the minivan but we ask her to make way for her younger
siblings—that's a chance to discuss humility. Each day offers
tons of chances to weave in virtuous formation."

Brandon and his wife of six years, Kathleen, look for
opportunities to foster growth in virtue within their family. "I like to set up potential moments of growth," Brandon
explained. "For example, if I want to instill patience in my
son, I'll give him a tedious task. If I want to encourage grat-

itude, I'll have him call up his grandma and thank her for something ordinary." For Brandon, having his children see *him* do those virtuous deeds is vital. "When our kids see us praying, they pray. When they see us serving each other before ourselves, they do the same. Since virtue is caught more often than taught, examples are deeply influential." Children mimic their parents' virtues *and* their vices, which makes virtuous living all the more important as spiritual heads and hearts of the family, especially in our modern day, when virtue is often scoffed at and vices are encouraged. For that reason, Brandon and Kathleen like to emphasize certain virtues that they feel are particularly important to hand onto their children, who are being raised in the midst of a secularist culture. Brandon divulged, "Three virtues we emphasize in particular are chastity, since our world idolizes sex; charity, since our culture hails individualism; and temperance, since we're encouraged to indulge without limit."

Growing in virtue as a leader is not without its challenges, especially with all of the commitments that daily work and family life requires. "The biggest challenge is inertia," Brandon mentioned. "Becoming virtuous is not something that happens naturally. You have to move, you have to actively pursue it. So many other tasks clamor for my attention and time." To help him overcome this hurdle, Brandon remembers St. John of the Cross' insight that we will be judged by our charity. "When we meet Christ after our deaths, we will not be judged by how much money we made, how far we advanced in our careers, or how well known we were. We'll be judged by our love. Did we help our spouse and children become saints or distract them from it?" So while the Vogts look for those ordinary chances to help their children grow in virtue, they also seek out those constant opportunities to grow in love themselves, becoming more perfect models of Christ and the Church for their family.

A Simple but Not-So-Easy Three-Step Process for Growing in Virtue

One of the spiritual leaders I admire is Dr. Edward Sri, husband, father of seven, and Catholic author and professor. Dr. Sri teaches these three steps, based on paragraph 1810 in the Catechism, as a simple and profound process for growing in virtue. Want to make your home a school of virtue like the homes of the spiritual leaders in this book? Here is your quick reference, step-by-step plan:

Education. Learn and teach about the virtues in your home. You also need to learn about vices, the opposites of the virtues, so you can detect when you are practicing those, instead of living the virtues. For example, pride, a capital vice (which means it leads to a host of other vices) can be tempered with humility. If you are a prideful person, it helps to learn about how to detect the sin of pride in yourself (for example, when you have the urge to be praised by others) and then learn how to work against it with its opposing virtue, humility (for example, by praying the "Litany of Humility"). When you take time to learn about virtue and vice, vocally teach these things to your family, too, prudently choosing the right way and the appropriate timing.

Practice. You can't just learn about the virtues and teach them to others. You have to live them! Growing in virtue takes deliberate, constant practice. Eliminate vices and purposefully replace them with virtues. Let's say you spend an inordinate amount of minutes wasting time on your smartphone. Instead of simply spending less time on your phone, replace that time with something else, something better, like playing with your kids. If you struggle with generosity, find ways to be generous by tithing more of your time, talent, or treasure.

Acquire grace. Pray for God to give you the grace to grow in virtue. Experience God's grace giving you strength to live virtuously and avoid vice through the power of the sacraments. You can't expect to grow in virtue without the grace of the Eucharist and the Sacrament of Confession. Strong spiritual leaders frequent the sacraments, along with their families, recognizing the wellspring of grace that exists in them. God wants to shower His grace on you, to give you the freedom and joy that comes from virtuous leadership and living.

The Secret to the School of Virtue: Wanting to Do It (and Then Doing It)

"I'm only qualified to give advice on how to teach virtue at home because it's something that we are striving for, not something that we've definitively accomplished," Meg Matanaer, wife and stay-at-home mother of five, ages seven and younger, confessed. "The biggest part of growing in virtue is simply wanting to do it."

Meg and her husband of eight years, Paul, a canon lawyer, also believe that virtue is most about living and leading by example. "My husband reminded me that God in His infinite wisdom designed the home as a school of virtue, *ipso facto*. Virtue will come naturally as we fulfill our duties that come with the territory," Meg reflected.

Meg and Paul, through "trial and pain, inclination and aspiration," as Meg states it, have a lot to teach others about spiritual leadership in the virtues:

Teach yourselves and your children to know what "the good" is and how to choose it. "True freedom is the capacity to choose the good. Do our kids know what the good is? Could they explain it to others? Are they convinced themselves? Could they choose it in difficult circumstances? This is what my husband and I are striving for, and it requires that both we and our children know the faith and engage in critical thinking."

Model and teach true masculinity and femininity. "For my little kids to develop their full sexual identity, they need to see true masculinity and femininity modeled in the family setting. Is Dad protecting and providing for the family? Is Mom loving and nurturing? Also, they need to see masculinity and femininity lived out in the religious life and priesthood. Ultimately, are they being properly formed in what it means to be a joyful man or woman of God? My husband and I try to avoid exposing them to anything that would hinder, distract, or slow down this process."

Among practicing other virtues, spiritual hearts should be patient, generous, and abounding in love and hope. "I think it's necessary for a mother to be faithful and prayerful, patient, kind, generous, strong, and really in love with her spouse and kids. I struggle with patience, in the moments when no one seems to be listening to me, and then when I step in something wet and the baby begins to cry and I notice that I never turned on the oven for dinner. And also in bigger things, like wanting a prayer answered, or for one of the kids to lose a bad habit, or with my own shortcomings. Most importantly, though, I think moms need to be women of prayer and hope. Many miracles have been worked in families due to the strength and courage of a mother's faithful prayers, and we should always remember what a powerful intercessor we can be for our loved ones. We've got Our Lady and St. Monica as beautiful examples of this."

Among practicing other virtues, spiritual heads should be zealous, courageous and sacrificial. "I married my husband because I knew that he would die for the truth. His zeal for the truth is such a blessing for our family, and it's a delight to watch him teach our kids the faith, always in a gentle, age-appropriate way. My children know that their dad is truly living out his Catholic faith every day—usually to the world's consternation—and what more could I hope for them than for them to know that my husband loves Our Lord so much that he would lay down his reputation at the foot of Christ's Cross, day in and day out?"

Family life poses plenty of challenges to growing in virtue, but strong spiritual leaders see those challenges as opportunities to practice virtue, whether that means being patient and loving in the midst of daily chaos or an argument, standing up for the truth when it's unpopular, protecting the innocence of children, or by giving up a personal desire to serve someone else's need. Spiritual leaders know that growing in virtue requires the desire, the will to grow in virtue, and then, over time and with intention, they give up a little of themselves with every virtuous act and become more like Christ.

Encouraging and Applauding Virtue in One Another

Leadership thrives on encouragement. When couples regularly acknowledge each other's strengths in leadership, spirituality, communication, affection, and other aspects of their relationship, those strengths grow even stronger. Conversely, when couples provide *too* much negative feedback (because some constructive criticism *is* necessary and good), personal growth can be stunted. Nothing can slow progress like feeling you're failing.

The Novecoskys deeply admire one another's virtues, and it inspires them to grow deeper in virtue themselves. "I admire her patience," Patrick, father of five, and publication director says of his wife, Michele. "She home schools our children, which takes a boatload of patience. We've been married for twelve years, but I learn something new about her and her virtues every day." Michele is also inspired by the virtue Patrick displays as the spiritual head of their family. "Order and perseverance are the virtues I admire most in my husband," she acknowledges. "He also encourages me and helps us to attend daily Mass and frequent Confession as a family, which strengthens my spiritual life."

Encourage your spouse when they are demonstrating sacrificial love for you, when you notice they are admirably patient in a given moment, when they shine a ray of hope into a seemingly hopeless situation. Regularly ask yourself, "What virtues can I encourage and applaud in my spouse? What virtues can I challenge them to grow in?" Further, encourage your children, too. Let them know when you see them living and making decisions virtuously, saying something like, "I noticed how patient you were with your brother when you were playing with the blocks today" to a young child, or, "I was very impressed with your prudent decision to leave that party" to a teenage son or daughter. You'll see more of what you acknowledge. In imitation of our heavenly Father, who loves to see us make progress in virtue, recognize and encourage that progress in your family members.

Infusing Family Life with Christian Culture

In addition to creating an atmosphere of virtue in our family life, as spiritual leaders we are given the opportunity to embrace Catholic culture in our homes. Catholic culture involves passing down a uniquely Christian way of living, based on values and traditions that find their origins in Christ and the early Church, a Church which Christ founded so as to continue handing on this unique culture long after He physically walked the earth. The two most important institutions we have in our world today—the family and the Church—were established by God so we could keep alive the way of life that God desires for us.

The rituals we have, the language we use, the practices we repeat, the stories we share—all of these things make up the concrete aspects of the Christian culture we inherit and pass on to our families. As Catholics we celebrate the Mass, we light candles, we pray with the Communion of Saints, we practice the sacraments, we speak using Scriptural language, we fast together, and we even have our own calendar of special feast days, helping to remind us of this common way of life that connects us to our fellow Christians, past and present, here and around the world, on earth and in heaven.

It is second nature for most of us to celebrate our spouse and children's birthdays, to watch fireworks on the Fourth of July, to gather together at every Thanksgiving around a big table garnished with a golden turkey and bowls heaping with cranberry sauce and stuffing. As spiritual leaders, we should place even higher priority on celebrating Catholic feast days and baptism anniversaries, living Advent and Lent in the home, and bringing our faith into family dinners and family meetings. Integrating these Christian cultural activities into our routines helps bring the Catholic faith to life in a vibrant way for our spouse and kids.

Creating an Environment Where Holiness Can Grow

The chief objective of infusing family life with Catholic culture is to create an environment where holiness can grow. To be holy means to be "set apart" for God, which often makes a home that is alive with Catholic culture look different from the homes around it. For the Staudts, they know they are achieving their goals when their family culture "goes against the flow" of secular culture, aiming to love God above everything else.

"We want our family to have a living relationship with God that permeates everything we do," observed Dr. Jared Staudt, husband, father, and theology professor. One of the primary ways that he and his wife, Anne, mother to their five children, work to make their Catholic faith shape their family life is by living and celebrating the Church's liturgical calendar in their own domestic church. "Living the liturgical seasons is important for us. We learn hymns for Advent and Lent. The kids can't wait to light the Advent Wreath, and they love hearing the story of salvation history as we put ornaments on the Jesse Tree. For Lent, we try to make it a truly penitential season for the whole family, eating more simply and trying to be a little more somber."

Anne elaborated with some additional cultural customs in their family. "We try to help them understand the meaning of the faith and we talk about stories from the Bible. For the kids' name days, the feast day of whichever saint's namesake they have, we allow them to pick something special that they want to eat or something that they would like to do. We light their baptismal candles on the anniversary of their baptisms. The kids love reading the lives of the saints and we try to follow up on that reading with examples of how we can imitate those saints." The Staudts also spend time teaching their young children about different vocations to which God may call them. "We want our children to have a lot of contact with priests and religious so that they can see good examples and models of religious life. We want our kids to know that they should listen for God's will and have courage in responding to it. We also talk about the importance of marrying the right person and how they can be holy in that vocation, too."

The climactic Catholic cultural event in the Staudt home, though, is Sunday Mass. "The way we dress for it, prepare for it, and respond to it afterward should show its central importance in grounding everything else that we do," Jared said. "The Eucharist is truly the heart of any Catholic culture, and we work to make the Eucharist the heart of our family."

For Jared and Anne, all of their efforts and activities to infuse their family life with Catholic culture stem from their desire to help their children know and love Christ. As Jared described, "Fostering holiness in ourselves and others is hard to do. It is a long process, and though we are not perfect parents, we hope that our children see that we love God more than anything else."

Spiritual Heads and Hearts Make Their Home a School of Virtue and Culture

The home has always been and still should be the primary school where men and women are formed into saints—persons with superior character, a common Christ-centered culture, and exceedingly beautiful virtue. *Every single one of us* has the capacity to make the home a blue ribbon school of virtue and culture; and as spiritual leaders, we actually have the *responsibility* to do so.

Spiritual leaders are called to look at education in their home in a unique way. Spiritual heads and hearts look at how they and their children are doing in the more important subjects of charity, self-donation, humility, generosity, patience, gratitude, peacefulness, receptivity, forgiveness, prayerfulness, and trust in God's will. They know that they are called to be models of virtue and infusers of culture for their families and that the payoff for doing this is great; in this school, the graduation party is in heaven.

Head to Head

"As much as fathers need to model the virtues for their children's sake, they need to model them for their own sake. Men need to know, too, that they can't do this alone. We're totally incapable of living a virtuous life on our own strength. We need God's help. That help comes through prayer, through a relationship with the Risen Christ. Once you begin—however imperfectly—

to pray and build your relationship with Jesus, you'll start to see amazing things happen. And you'll stumble. We all do. But when you do, know that you're not alone. Ask Him for help and say, 'Jesus, I trust in you!'"

—*Patrick Novecosky,*
husband and father, publications director

Heart to Heart

"Think big (I want my family and me to become saints!) and start small. We can't suddenly jump to Mother Teresa's level of prayer or service or become little like St. Thérèse in a day, but we can be faithful to little things, like five minutes of prayer a day, or being loving with our kids when we're zipping up their coats before sending them off to school, or giving our husbands hugs when they come home from work. All these little things will eventually get us to where we want to be heading. There is, unfortunately, no short cut on the path to holiness."

—*Meg Matenaer,*
wife and mother

Your Leadership Action Steps

Beginner
Pick one of the cardinal or theological virtues mentioned in the chapter and learn more about that virtue this month. (For example, if you pick hope, you can read verses in Scripture that encourage hope, stories of saints who had hope in God's will and hope for heaven, etc.)

Intermediate
Re-read the section, "A Simple but Not-So-Easy Three-Step Process for Growing in Virtue." Then, on a piece of paper

or on a note in your phone, write "Education, Practice, Acquire Grace." Pick a virtue that you want to improve on this month, and then take time each day to learn about that virtue (by reading the Catechism, verses in the Bible that pertain to the virtue, stories of saints who practiced the virtue, or articles about the virtue from great websites like Good-Confession.com), practice the virtue, and pray for God to give you the grace to grow in that virtue. Make sure you put your reminder note in a prominent place to encourage your virtue education, practice, and prayer each day.

Advanced

Re-read the section, "Seeking Ordinary Opportunities and Moments of Growth." Discuss with your spouse three virtues that you want your family to exemplify. Write them down and look for opportunities to encourage those virtues every day in your own life and in the lives of your other family members, especially over the next month. Take advantage of those moments for growth by taking some action every day—even if its small—to practice one of those virtues. (For example, if you want gratitude to be an exemplary virtue in your family, write and mail a thank you note to someone whose friendship you are thankful for, and have each member of the family do the same.)

6

They Take Up Their Cross

"If any man would come after me,
let him deny himself and take up
his cross daily and follow me."
—Luke 9:23

Leading When Life Gets Hard

Family life brings countless joys and blessings, but it also comes with many crosses, large and small, that ebb and flow throughout the seasons of our lives. Every family is carrying crosses—struggles with fertility, physical and mental illnesses and disabilities, addictions, unemployment, family members doubting or drifting away from faith, or marital strife, along with all of the other crosses that descend upon our everyday lives, like getting stuck in traffic on the way to an important event or trying to parent rowdy kids while your patience slowly diminishes.

Family life is hard, but true leaders distinguish themselves as such by the way they handle crises of all shapes and sizes, taking up the very real crosses that are presented to them, and calling on the Lord to strengthen them when they are weak. Modeling themselves after Christ, the Suffering Servant, we find in them what I refer to as "suffering leaders," who recognize that to truly imitate and follow Jesus, their leadership must be strong when leading is hard to do.

Special Needs, Special Leadership

"Every cross we bear is a blessing in disguise, although we rarely see our challenges in this light when we are experiencing them," reflected Randy Hain, husband, father of two, and Catholic author and speaker. It was through a cross that Randy and his wife of twenty years, Sandra, experienced one of the greatest blessings in their life—their family's conversion to Catholicism.

"I think our son's diagnosis of autism when he was twenty-seven months old was the catalyst that eventually led our entire family into the Catholic Church in 2006," Randy recalls. "We had no faith at the time of his diagnosis, and our focus was on simply giving him the care and therapies he needed to function in the world. Our second son was born in 2001, and our marriage grew stronger as we kept our lives focused on giving our children and each other the love and support we all needed to get through those challenging early years of the diagnosis. We eventually moved in 2005 to be closer to our son's therapists and my work, which led to a series of life-changing events and our eventual conversion into the Catholic Church the following year."

Of course, their Catholic faith brought them consolation and strength, but the Hains still felt the weight of the crosses in their lives. Their focus, however, shifted when a priest challenged them to embrace their son's diagnosis in a new way.

"In response to learning that we pray every day about our oldest son's future and that he be healed of his autism, a priest at my parish encouraged us to pray first for the ability to fully accept the beautiful gift of our child exactly as God created him. Reflecting on this has made me realize how often, without thinking, I ask God for His help in improving situations and solving problems. Instead of praying for acceptance and discernment about what lessons God wants to teach me or the blessings hidden in these challenges, I had been seeking to reshape the issues into something more pleasing to me instead of pleasing to Him."

Randy now looks for the redemptive power in all of the crosses that he carries in his life, recognizing that although it can be difficult to see blessings in suffering, uniting one's suffering with Christ on the Cross and offering it up allows a person to "radically recalibrate" his mindset and form a deeper trust in God. Trials become opportunities to glorify God, grow in virtue, and strengthen spiritual leadership in the home.

"Without a doubt, our gifted child and his presence in our lives opened my heart and was a significant catalyst behind our joining the Catholic Church and the strong faith our family has today," Randy revealed. "I believe our son's autism has helped my wife and me focus on what is truly important. We don't waste our energies on wishing for a different life or buying things we don't need. We don't argue about silly things. We have learned to support and pray for each other when our challenges are greatest, and our love has grown stronger over the years. Raising our son with autism can sometimes be exhausting, but we never feel resentment. We see him as God's gift to us, and I assure you, the blessings far exceed the challenges."

Randy has learned that taking up his cross is one of his most important tasks as the spiritual head of his family. For the Hains, every cross is an opportunity to learn and grow and persevere. "My wife and I use our life challenges as teaching moments for our children and ourselves. Instead of complaining, we seek out the Blessed Mother's intercession. Instead of feeling hopeless, we ask the Lord for His

strength and the courage to face our problems. We pray together as a family and take turns asking for God's help and
blessing for our individual burdens, but more importantly
for the burdens of others. My wife and I believe strongly that
if our children see us on our knees in prayer, thanking God
for our blessings and sincerely asking for His help, they are
much more likely to do the same when they have families of
their own."

Take Up Your Cross and Follow Me

You are not alone if in the midst of suffering in your personal
or family life you have turned to God, and in tears, in anger, or in desperation, asked "Why?" It is easy to feel aban-
doned and spiritually emptied when suffering comes barging
through the door of your life. God never said that our lives
would be easy or that our families would be perfect, but He
did assure us that we would not be alone as we face the trib-
ulations we endure.

Laury Beesley, founder and president of the non-profit
organization Widows GPS, and mother to two grown children, lost her husband Jeff in 2007. She is no stranger to the
immense pain that comes from carrying a cross that seems
almost too heavy to bear. But, she mentioned, "Turning to
God brings you the strength and courage to go on." Laury
elaborated, "After receiving so much love and support from
fellow Catholics, our parish church, our pastor, and other Christians (two in particular who became Catholic after
Jeff's death), I gained enough strength to want to help others
who have been widowed." Laury now commits her time to
providing guidance, power, and support (GPS) for widows
and widowers, reminding them—as she continues to remind
herself—that no one is ever alone in carrying a cross.

When Jesus came into our world, He also came into our
suffering. He is no stranger to pain, and He willingly accom-

panies us in our trials, holding our hands in our moments of brokenness, rejection, abuse, betrayal, sickness, and shame. And He gives us His Word, to strengthen us for the suffering we endure:

- We are children of God, and if children, then heirs, heirs of God and fellow heirs with Christ, provided we suffer with him in order that we may also be glorified with him. I consider that the sufferings of this present time are not worth comparing with the glory that is to be revealed to us (Rom 8:16–18).

- We are afflicted in every way, but not crushed; perplexed, but not driven to despair; persecuted, but not forsaken; struck down, but not destroyed; always carrying in the body the death of Jesus, so that the life of Jesus may also be manifested in our bodies (2 Cor 4:8–10).

- More than that, we rejoice in our sufferings, knowing that suffering produces endurance, and endurance produces character, and character produces hope, and hope does not disappoint us, because God's love has been poured into our hearts through the Holy Spirit which has been given to us (Rom 5:3–5).

- 'He will wipe away every tear from their eyes, and death shall be no more, neither shall there be mourning nor crying nor pain any more, for the former things have passed away.' And he who sat upon the throne said, 'Behold, I make all things new' (Rev 21:4–5).

"Offering It Up"

God does not let our suffering go to waste. He allows us to share in its redemptive value when we offer it up and unite our crosses with His Cross, for the building up of the body of Christ. But how, practically, do spiritual leaders "offer it up"?

Begin the day with the Morning Offering. My family re-cites this prayer every morning before my husband heads to work and we begin our day: "O Jesus, through the Immaculate Heart of Mary, I offer You my prayers, works, joys and sufferings of this day for all the intentions of Your Sacred Heart, in union with the Holy Sacrifice of the Mass throughout the world, in reparation for my sins, for the intentions of all my relatives and friends, and in particular for the intentions of the Holy Father."

Informally ask God throughout the day to use your sufferings, as they occur, for good. You could say something as simple as, "Lord, I offer this frustration I'm feeling for the consolation of my friend Jenny who is battling cancer" or "I offer the annoyance of this flu for the strengthening of my spouse's spiritual leadership." In addition to asking God to apply the merits of your suffering to an intention close to your heart, you can also pray that He will use them as He or His mother sees fit, for the good of the Church.

Follow St. Thérèse of Lisieux's practice of using "sacrifice beads." These can be made or purchased and consist of a string of ten beads with a crucifix at one end that remind us of our call to take up our crosses and follow Christ, and a medal of St. Thérèse on the other end that reminds us of the importance of following her "little way" of spirituality. Keep the beads in your pocket and, secretly, when you mentally and prayerfully offer up something to God, in union with Christ's sufferings on the Cross, slide one of the beads toward the crucifix.

Christ's command to "take up your cross daily and follow me" has a happy ending. Remember that Christ's Passion and death—the greatest evil and suffering our world has ever seen—was followed by the Resurrection. Christ's own life shows us that suffering is not an end in itself and that we can always look ahead to brighter days, most fully in the glory of heaven, when resurrected joy will be all that we know and suffering will be a distant memory.

"I Just Wish God Didn't Trust Me So Much!"

"Late at night, when I cannot seem to shut my brain off and sleep does not come easily, I frequently find solace in the words of Mother Teresa, who said, 'I know God won't give me anything I can't handle. I just wish He didn't trust me so much.' I believe there are lessons in life that we sometimes learn with great difficulty," Dana Mooney, wife and speech-language pathologist, explained.

One of those difficult lessons came in the form of a cross for Dana and her husband Teague, an electrical engineer, during their first few years of marriage. "Being a cradle Catholic, I have grown up surrounded by the love of the Church. I have been very blessed in my life with a wonderful family, a loving husband, and an amazing job doing what I really love. Due to all of these things, faith has been easy, many times effortless, and unfortunately, at times, taken for granted. Not until I began to struggle with my health and fertility did I experience a true test of faith," Dana continued.

During graduate school, Dana started experiencing bouts of extreme anxiety, along with insomnia and erratic mood changes. Shortly after, there followed changes in her menstrual cycle that didn't go away with time and decreased stress, as her doctor had originally predicted.

"I continued to pray about these struggles and began consulting other physicians. Day in and day out I was met with thoughts of doubt, sadness, and at times, anger. Why was this happening to me? What had I done to deserve these struggles? Why was it that individuals who willingly select abortion were given the amazing gift of co-creating new life that I may never have? I made myself sick and crazy over these thoughts. I remember, specifically, one night that I felt the deepest sadness and most intense anxiety and began to cry uncontrollably. Teague held me and urged me to trust in God, reminding me that everything would work out the way it is intended to. At the time, I rejected and resented his 'everything's fine' attitude."

Later, in the stillness of the adoration chapel, before Jesus in the Blessed Sacrament, Dana felt a shift in her heart and in her thinking. "Rather than fervently asking, 'Why me?' 'Why us?' or 'How come *they* get to?,' I realized my questions should lift my eyes and heart from myself to focus on God. In focusing on the wonderful gifts He has given me rather than the difficulties I have endured, a light came into my life that has opened my eyes to the greatness of His love. My health has continued to be an uphill battle, and still some days I have difficulty standing under the weight of this cross. But in the times I cannot find the strength to stand, it is then that I know I must kneel."

Dana and Teague believe that their roles as the spiritual head and spiritual heart of their family are still critically important, even without children in the home at this time in their lives. "Often times, people view spiritual leadership as something you have the responsibility to exercise when you have kids; but really, couples without children are meant to be spiritual leaders for each other, too—helping lead one another to heaven," explained Teague. Dana and Teague recognize that sometimes God works through *spiritual* parenthood—not only physical, biological parenthood—as a means to strengthen his spiritual leaders.

The Mooneys try to lead each other toward a greater trust in God and in His plan for their lives and their family. "My Catholic faith is always helping me through these times whether I realize it or not," Teague, a convert to Catholicism in 2010, noted. "The roots of my optimism lay in my trust and faith that God is there to help us get through whatever we are going through, as long as we hold onto that trust and faith in Him."

What God Did When I Thought My Crosses Were Too Small

Every Lent, I resume my favorite Lenten prayer tradition, praying for a different person, couple, or family on each of the forty days. I offer all of my prayers, petitions, frustrations, joys, and sufferings on the specified day for their intentions. It was a particularly impactful experience for me one year. Before the Lenten season, I had become unusually fixated on the fact that the crosses in my life at the time seemed to be so small compared to the challenges that so many of my acquaintances, friends, and family were facing, and I allowed this confusion and despair for the pains of others to plague my mood for days and weeks.

Then God did something. Over forty days, He showed me that I was looking at crosses in terms of "mine" and "theirs," when I should have been looking at them as "ours." The petitions that poured in from friends and relatives over six weeks stirred my heart and dominated my thoughts and prayers each day, bringing me to a better understanding of how crosses are meant to be carried—together.

How easy it is for me to get caught up in my own little world, focusing on my crosses, however big or small I think they are, not realizing that my neighbor's cross *is* my cross and that I am meant to help carry it. After that Lenten season came to an end, I realized that this prayer practice could not. It had changed me, making me more acutely aware of my connection to others as part of the Body of Christ. We are called to be there for our brothers and sisters in Christ, yet often we may fail to pray for others when we say we will, or we are so focused on our own needs and petitions that we act as if we don't have time to intercede for anyone else's. When this happens, we miss out on the purifying treasure of shouldering the weight of other's burdens and lightening each other's loads. We lose the opportunity to help each other become stronger spiritual leaders.

Here's how you can participate in your own cross-sharing mission:

- When a person you know pops into your head for whatever reason, reach out to them and ask them how you can pray for them that day.
- If you have a friend or relative asking you for prayers for some intention, think of how you can relieve some of their burden, not only through your prayers, but also through an act of service—gifting them with a meal, an inspirational book, a cup of coffee, a listening ear, a hug, or a thoughtful card.
- Challenge yourself to offer not only your vocal prayers, but also your daily sufferings, frustrations, accomplishments, and joys for another. For example, when you start to get annoyed as you are stuck in traffic, offer your frustration for your special prayer recipient. No negative or positive feeling or experience, when offered for another, is ever wasted. God is meticulous in applying the fruits of our prayer to those in need.

You are not alone on this sometimes exhausting, challenging journey of spiritual leadership and family life. Reach out to others who are suffering, and allow them to reach out to you. When I thought my crosses were too small, God repositioned my outlook—shaking up my spiritual life and giving me bigger crosses to help carry—and I better understood how taking up a cross, whether it's mine or a small part of someone else's, is a channel of grace for all those suffering.

Spiritual Heads and Hearts Take Up Their Cross and Follow Christ

After learning from and observing many of the spiritual leaders I admire, I uncovered a big difference between them and others who do not see spiritual leadership as a privilege or responsibility in their lives. Both groups of people are given crosses to carry, often very heavy ones. But the strong spiritual leaders take up their cross, and then they follow Christ. The second part of that Bible verse is perhaps the most important. Taking up our crosses is only part of the equation. After recognizing and accepting the crosses in our lives, we are faced with a choice: to carry it while heading toward or away from Christ.

When we choose to run toward God, even in our darkest moments, we discover that suffering brings us deeper into the mystery of His life, where suffering is not the final word. Resurrection is. Glory is. Eternal love and joy is. Strong spiritual leaders believe, even if their feelings don't always coincide perfectly with that belief, that suffering is a path to holiness.

"If God sends you many **sufferings**, it is a sign that He has great **plans** for you and certainly wants to make you a **saint**."

—St. Ignatius Loyola

Head to Head

"I struggle with the same challenges and crosses others face and I don't pretend to have all of the answers. Yet, I do know that it is not too late to place our relationships with God, our wives, and our children on a proper footing with our priorities in this order: Christ

96   **HEAD AND HEART**

first, family second, and work third. Are we prepared to do what is necessary to make this happen? Are we ready to bear the crosses we have been given? I have long been drawn to St. Joseph and find in his life the encouragement to be more obedient and trusting in God's promises. I pray for his intercession and reflect on his courageous example in caring for Jesus and Mary. If we can emulate St. Joseph even a little each day, we will be that much closer to becoming the men we are called to be."

—Randy Hain,
husband and father,
president and founder of Serviam Partners

Heart to Heart

"Throughout my childhood, there was a phrase my mother often used in our household whenever my sisters or I were experiencing something difficult, and to this day, every time I face a challenge I can hear her voice saying, 'Offer it up.' As a teenager, I looked at this as her way of saying, 'Just deal with it.' As I entered adulthood, I looked at my mom's words in a new light. 'Offer it up'—offer it into God's hands, and praise Him for the blessings in your life. God offered up His only Son for us. What greater sacrifice is there? I have encountered some trying times, but I have found the greatest peace in picking up my cross, whatever it may be, and offering my pain, sorrow, joy, and praise to God."

—Dana Mooney,
wife and speech language pathologist

Your Leadership Action Steps

Beginner

What cross are you carrying in your life right now? Are you embracing it, offering it up, or are you running from God and from this cross? Write down your commitment to uniting your suffering with Jesus, asking Him to give you strength to carry this cross.

Intermediate

Re-read the section, "Offering It Up." Every day this week (and hopefully thereafter), begin each day with the Morning Offering. Also, consider implementing the practice of the sacrifice beads, encouraging your family members to participate as well.

Advanced

This month, begin participating in your own "cross-sharing mission" as described in the section titled, "What God Did When I Thought My Crosses Were Too Small." Make sure to incorporate all three bulleted suggestions into your routine and consider journaling your experience after the month goes by.

7

They Cultivate Peace

"For peace is a good so great,
that even in this earthly and mortal life
there is no word we hear with such pleasure,
nothing we desire with such zest,
or find to be more thoroughly gratifying."
—St. Augustine, City of God

Is Peace Still A 'Thing' in Our Society?

Cultivating peace is my biggest struggle in my own quest to be a stronger spiritual leader for my family. Every single day, I wrestle the demon of anxiety, and I often lose. It's disheartening. It's demotivating. But the good news—the news that I have to remind my broken, stressed self every time I fall—is that God did not create stress. He, as the Lord of peace, the wellspring of balance, restfulness and hope, wants to give us a future unhindered by the anxieties of this life. He wants to free me—and you—from the stress that plagues our personal joy and our ability to spiritually lead our families well.

For a long time, I bought into the lie that anxiety was an irritating relative that I was stuck with for the rest of my life, and that peace was not really a 'thing' in our culture anymore. Witnessing leaders that I admire find peace amidst the chaos of modern family life brought me hope that I didn't have to wait until heaven to get a taste of the contentedness my heart longs for. I was awed by the notion that some of these ordinary men and women actually experience a deep-rooted sense of peace and calm, even while living with houses full of kids to care for, careers to pursue, chores to complete, and a host of other pressing responsibilities to manage.

It may be hard to believe that peace of mind, heart, and home is still capable of being grasped in our lives today when we look at our packed Google calendars, listen to constant background noise, sit in traffic jams, and question whether our smartphones are an additional appendage to our bodies. But God is so much bigger than the stress we allow in our lives, and He wants to transform us as spiritual heads and hearts to be living, breathing leaders and lovers of peace. By taking prayerful and practical steps to cultivate peace, we help ourselves and our families achieve the other leadership characteristics in this book, not in frenzy but in confident calm.

Downsize and Simplify

Since my own parents were (and still are) remarkable spiritual leaders for my family, they gave my two younger sisters and me the foundational tools we needed to aspire to become strong spiritual hearts in our own future families, beginning what I hope will be a spiritual legacy that will ripple into future generations.

As I have already mentioned, cultivating peace is not my forte—nor is it my father's. But watching my dad over the years not only work to cultivate peace but *struggle* to cultivate peace has deeply affected me. My father, Tom Peterson, husband, father of three adult girls, and president and founder of the apostolates Catholics Come Home and VirtueMedia, discovers more peace in his life by making bold gestures to allow God to flood his life with grace. One of those bold gestures happened in 1998, the year my dad began his jour-

ney of cultivating peace, the year he felt called by the Holy
Spirit to "downsize and simplify."

"There was a time in my life when God had a relatively
small place in my heart," admitted Tom. "In the 1990s, when
my career was taking off, I wasn't feeling much peace, and I
certainly wasn't very happy. I began to think that there must
be more to life than this." When Tom examined his lifestyle,
he discovered all sorts of obstacles blocking his path to God,
to spiritually leading his family, and to finding authentic happiness. "Upon beginning my lucrative corporate career out
of college, I was goal-oriented, but self-centered and materi-
alistic. During that time in my life, God and His abounding
peace floated more into the background."

Everything changed when Tom's heart was converted on
a retreat during Eucharistic Adoration. "It was as if God was
saying to me, 'You've got one foot in my world and one in the
secular world. It's time to choose sides, Tom. Come, follow
me. *Downsize and simplify.*' I began downsizing my ego and
simplifying everything in my life. I shed the extra baggage I
was carrying to make room for God's love and peace in my
life. By the grace of God, He opened the door to me using
my gifts for His glory, and for the first time in years, with less
stuff, more God, and more focus on being a spiritual leader
for my family, my heart was at peace. Even now, years after
that transformative time in my life, I continue to ask God for
wisdom to downsize and simplify areas of my life that keep
me from growing in faith and finding peace, knowing that
where my treasure is, there will my heart be also."

Equally moving is my mom's example of searching for
and achieving peace as the spiritual heart of her family. For
Tricia, Tom's wife of twenty-eight years, cultivating peace
is all about small, but meaningful steps toward greater
peace every single day, and in all of the trying moments
in between.

"My goal as a mother is to be a model of holiness for my children. So when they see me maintaining peace in my own life, they too will be able to learn how to search for it and experience it as well," Tricia reflected. "Jesus said, 'Peace I leave with you, my peace I give to you.' What a beautiful gift! If we can remind ourselves to use this gift of peace, our daily problems would be so much easier to endure and our families would flourish."

But peace isn't always easy to maintain, especially in the midst of struggles of all shapes and sizes within the family. "As a wife and mother, the greatest threat to my peace is when problems, sadness, or hurts affect my husband or children. Their heartaches are my heartaches," Tricia explained. "My best weapon is prayer. I also regularly refer to a little book called *Searching for and Maintaining Peace* by Fr. Jacques Philippe, which reminds me that it is the devil's desire to steal my peace, and that knowledge alone gives me the power to fight for it so he doesn't win."

For Tricia, practicing peace in her life and family comes down to one crucial, repeated decision: to trust. "The greatest lesson God has taught me about peace is to trust Him! I have learned through some very difficult times that no matter the outcome of a struggle I am going through, God will get me through it. He loves me so much; I am *His* child. It is really quite an amazing feeling to be at peace in the midst of a struggle, but that's what trust can do. It can turn our weakness into His strength, His promise and gift of peace."

Honoring the Lord's Day: The Foundation of Personal and Family Peace

I have learned from some of the strongest examples of spiritual leaders in my life, in addition to more error than trial in my own experience, that 'keeping holy the sabbath' is foundational for cultivating peace of heart and home, as well as transforming one's spiritual leadership.

Many of us know the Third Commandment given by God to Moses: "Remember the sabbath day, to keep it holy. Six days you shall labor, and do all your work; but the seventh day is a sabbath to the Lord your God; . . . therefore the Lord blessed the sabbath day and hallowed it" (Ex 20:8–11).

Unfortunately, knowing the commandment doesn't mean it is well practiced. Full schedules, sports events and TV, open restaurants and shopping malls, and a general cultural habit of working too much and playing too little make it easy to let Sundays pass us by as just another day of the week. But God was clear: the sabbath—which, thanks to the Resurrection of Jesus Christ, Christians now celebrate on Sunday—is altogether different. Furthermore, as Christians, we look at Sunday as the first day of the week, not the last. The Catechism explains, "For Christians it has become the first of all days, the first of all feasts, the Lord's Day . . . Sunday" (2174). Reveling in the peace of the Resurrection is supposed to be the way in which we *start* the week off on the right foot, with a sense of rejuvenated rest, having devoted the day to prayer, play, thanksgiving, remembrance of God's covenant with His people, and, most importantly, communal worship in the Holy Mass.

Voltaire, eighteenth-century French philosopher and well-known attacker of Catholicism, once wrote, "If you want to kill Christianity, you must abolish Sunday." Where the sabbath rest and worship is forgotten, a weak to non-existent practice of Christianity can almost inevitably be found. Conversely, those who take their spiritual leadership in the family seriously know that Sunday is the key to personal and family peace, the lifeblood of Christian life in the home. Prioritizing Sunday worship and rest takes patience and intention.

> Sanctifying Sundays and holy days requires a common effort. Every Christian should avoid making unnecessary demands on others that would hinder them from observing the Lord's Day. Traditional activities (sport, restaurants, etc.), and social necessities (public services, etc.), require some people to work on Sundays, but everyone should still take care to set aside sufficient time for leisure. (CCC 2187)

Spiritual leaders exert the effort to keep holy the Lord's Day in their homes in unique and various ways, including:

- Refraining from shopping
- Fasting from media (either all day or during certain hours)
- Getting the most out of Mass by going over the readings as a family and later discussing what they took away from Mass that day through the Scriptures, homily, or personal prayer
- Reserving time for naps or pleasure reading
- Cooking a big family meal together
- Playing games or watching a movie as a family
- Holding a family meeting
- Taking a day trip
- Spending time outdoors hiking or playing in the backyard or at a park
- Getting together with good family friends or extended relatives
- Gathering around the family altar or prayer space for intercessory prayer and spiritual reading and reflection
- Celebrating feast days with special activities or food related to the holy day
- Doing favorite hobbies individually or collectively
- Saying a family Rosary

- Serving the poor and others in need in the community
- Participating in parish ministries or gatherings
- Visiting sick friends or relatives
- Initiating or joining in a service project
- In general, keeping all of the various idols at bay that try to take God's place on Sunday, whatever those idols may be

As the spiritual head or heart of your home, you can customize your Lord's Day activities and celebrations for your family, remembering that the goal is worship, rest, and leisure.

If we aren't careful, we run the risk of leading our families into a habit of glorifying work and diminishing leisure, which Catholic philosopher Josef Pieper contends is the foundation of all culture. In his masterful work, *Leisure: The Basis of Culture*, Pieper contends that leisure requires constant affirmation by our practice of it and leads us to an inner joyfulness that lasts. "This is why the ability to be 'at leisure' is one of the basic powers of the human soul . . . the power to be at leisure is the power to step beyond the working world and win contact with those superhuman, life-giving forces that can send us, renewed and alive again, into the busy world of work." Leisure makes us more *spiritual* leaders, by bringing us in close contact with the God who made us for rest, not for toil. Work is a means to an end, and that end is leisure, first here on earth, and ultimately in the great festivity of the heavenly banquet, where stillness and joy and rest and worship meet and converge into the peace that all of our hearts were made for.

Peace Can Live Wherever Your Family Is

"Devin and I married in 2006 and eagerly looked forward to the blessing of many children and a happy home," recounted Katie Rose, Devin's wife of eight years and mother of two. "Instead, our Lord blessed us with incredible suffering in those first years of marriage, including three failed adoptions, three miscarriages, lots of NaPro (Natural Procreative Technology) fertility treatments, and, ultimately, one C-section hysterectomy. So after the very happy birth of our daughter in 2012, Devin and I felt like we just wanted to heal. We wanted to be a quiet family, raise chickens, write books, and drink good tea. We bought ten acres in the Texas hills and felt like we were sailing into a safe harbor where we could put down roots and raise our two children."

Then, Katie explained, "irony and spiritual growth" entered the picture, bringing them face to face with a different reality than the peace they expected to find in rural farm life. "We had taken the gift of peace into our own hands. The reality, however, was that our farm was terribly lonely. We had no supportive community of faith. Our Catholic friends were all in the city, forty miles away. So, while Devin and I sought peace on our little Catholic homestead, what we actually had was emptiness. Too much silence, not enough peace." It was actually when Devin, a professional software developer, and Katie moved back to town, near a bustling parish, that they found the peace—and the community— they were longing for.

Now, instead of searching for the perfect place to find peace, the Roses attempt to create the right atmosphere and lifestyle that promote peace in their home. Some of these peace-cultivating practices for them include:

Moderating noise and distraction. For Devin and Katie's family, this means spending more time outside, reading books, and playing together. The couple also tries to keep their Internet and smartphone usage, as well as news consumption, in check.

Designating a prayer space in the home. "We have reserved one of the bedrooms in our home as a family chapel," Katie mentioned, observing that this place facilitates more family prayer time. "We have the Stations of the Cross and religious art on the walls, and the room seems to breathe with prayerful silence; it smells like candles and has a holy water font, and I often find my children in there, looking at the Stations and trying to make sense of what they see."

Guarding silence and unscheduled time. Katie articulated, "The city is filled with noise of all sorts. I consider it an important part of my ministry as a mother to guard silence and unscheduled time in our home. If Christ is our peace, then we need to make room for Him through silence and unstructured time for reflection."

Maintaining personal balance and rest. By maintaining their own health and energy levels, the Roses maximize their ability to serve their family and experience personal and familial peace. Katie does this by getting sufficient sleep, making time for daily prayer or Mass, eating healthfully, taking naps, enlisting outside help with housecleaning, and keeping a cheerful attitude. "When my maternal stress grows, so does the level of conflict and tantrums in my home; in order to grow peace in my family, I must care properly for myself."

Trying to keep work stress out of the home. "I used to become stressed about work frequently," Devin admitted, "But now I decide to leave work at work. When I come home, if I am still mentally dealing with some issue, I talk to my wife about it and we work through it. It often helps just to have someone to talk to. If I need to vent more, I call up a friend who knows the situation and can sympathize."

Devin and Katie also find more margins of peace in their home by fostering mutual respect among family members, living in the present moment, and frequenting the sacraments. These simple, but intentional steps that the Rose family takes to cultivate more peace in their home foster a deep sense of fulfillment in their daily lives and contribute to the strengthening of their roles as spiritual head and heart, drawing them closer to Jesus, whose presence is more noticeable to peaceful souls. "And the peace of God, which passes all understanding, will keep your hearts and your minds in Christ Jesus" (Phil 4:7).

Peace Destroyers and Builders for Spiritual Leadership

Spiritual leaders are intentional about practicing habits that build peace in their lives, while working to avoid habits that actively work against cultivating peace. Here are some of the peace destroyers and builders that spiritual leaders have uncovered, which you can use to your advantage in the process of growing as a more peaceful spiritual head or heart of your family.

Peace Destroyers

An overly busy life. Socrates is believed to have warned, "Beware the barrenness of a busy life." Having one's hands full is different than being busy. Fill your hands with the right things—fulfilling work, meaningful hobbies, purposeful extracurricular activities, service to others, rearing of children! Don't let time pass you by because you are saying yes to all the wrong things and no to all the right ones.

Constant noise. "God speaks in the silence of the heart," Blessed Mother Teresa reminded. If there is constant noise in our lives, we can't hear God speaking to us and directing us toward a greater sense of peace in our leadership and lives.

Suffering (and the fear of it). Pain and the fear of pain can be crippling—spiritually, emotionally, mentally, and physically consuming. When we see suffering as an end, and not as a road that leads to redemption, peace has no room to be in the picture.

Stress over daily living and tough decisions. Money and the other troubles of day-to-day life or difficult decisions we have to make threaten to take more control over our peace than they deserve—which is none.

Sin. A habit of sin and unrepentance is one of the greatest peace-killers in our lives. When we turn in on ourselves (that's what sin is: selfishness), we push God away, the source of all peace.

Fixation on our own faults and the faults of others. Focusing too heavily on your or others' faults is sure to wreck your peace. We too often ruminate over the splinters and logs in everyone's eyes, including our own.

Relationships that drain. Relationships that tear us down, rather than build us up, have the same tearing-down effect on our peace. This is why choosing the right relationships (friends) and working hard to improve the right relationships (like with spouses and family members) is so important to maintaining peace.

One of my favorite spiritual writers, Fr. Jacques Philippe, writes in his simple and powerful treatise, *Searching For and Maintaining Peace*: "All the reasons that cause us to lose our sense of peace are bad reasons." And they are. These are all bad reasons to lose your peace. God wants to free you from these peace destroyers and leave you instead with *His* all-encompassing, unshakable peace. "Peace I leave with you; my peace I give to you; not as the world gives do I give to you. Let not your hearts be troubled, neither let them be afraid" (Jn 14:27).

Peace Builders

Prayer and worship. When you create intentional space for God *every single day*, you simultaneously make room for peace.

Leisure. Time for play, celebration, and relaxation are not only the basis of culture in the broadest sense of the term, but also the basis for your leadership and family culture.

Abandonment to God's will. Letting things be out of your control and in God's is a game-changer for maintaining peace in your life. Hand your anxieties to Him, remembering His yoke is easy and His burden light.

Patience with others and with ourselves. Inching closer to perfection (sanctity) takes a great deal of time. St. Francis de Sales said that "nothing retards progress in a virtue so much as wanting to acquire it with too much haste." But with patience, progress in virtue and in cultivating lasting peace can be achieved.

The sacraments. Thank God for the sacraments, especially for the privilege of being able to regularly receive Jesus—the source of all peace—in the Holy Eucharist, and to recommit ourselves to peace when we fall far from it through the Sacrament of Confession. (Learn more about this at GoodConfession.com.)

Spiritual reading. If we are serious about cultivating peace, we have to make an effort to learn about how to continuously build on it, and spiritual reading helps us do that. (See the epilogue for reading resources.)

Living in the present moment. Catholic convert from Judaism Francois-Marie-Jacob Libermann advised, "Be docile and pliable in the hands of God." To do this, we have to be comfortable allowing God to form us and lead us in the present moment, and be unmoved by mistakes of the past or concerns of the future.

> "I have said this to you, that in me you may have **peace**. In the world you have **tribulation**; but be of good **cheer**, I have overcome the world."
>
> —John 16:33

Spiritual Heads and Hearts Cultivate Peace

Spiritual giants throughout the centuries and in our present day agree that God acts in the soul that is at peace. If you desire to be a strong spiritual leader for your family, you have to earnestly and wholeheartedly search for peace and work to maintain it in your personal and family life. When you intentionally cultivate peace, God will move mountains in your life and in your family. All the other leadership traits you have been working on will settle comfortably into place. You will begin to experience the satisfying of that craving we all have for peace in our hearts and in our homes. And this leads to fulfillment in our roles as the spiritual heads and hearts that God called us to be, not only for His glory, but for our own happiness, too.

Head to Head

"With our families at peace, we are able to hear God better and follow His plan for us. Seek out other men, probably older than yourself, who exhibit these qualities. See how they discipline their children, how they show affection for their children, how they treat their spouse. Emulate in your own family the good things they do, or consider how you may adapt them to your own particular needs. Finally, you must yourself have peace from God to help others receive that peace. Seek out a solid priest to be your spiritual director. Talk to him about what you struggle with as a father, and listen to his wisdom."

—*Devin Rose, husband and father, professional software developer, and Catholic apologist*

Heart to Heart

"Peace is attainable! But in order to demonstrate peace to our families, we must first learn how to cultivate it in ourselves. Years ago, my pastor suggested that I find a Bible verse and repeat it over and over again when I was struggling. I would repeat 'Love is patient, love is kind' almost daily as I was raising my children. As wives and mothers, we need to emulate peace in our homes so our families can learn how to find peace in their struggles. By doing so, we teach our children to trust in God's promise that He will always take care of us."

—Tricia Peterson,
wife and mother

Your Leadership Action Steps

Beginner

Like Tricia mentioned in her "Heart to Heart" advice, find a Bible verse that helps cultivate in you a spirit of peace. Write it down on a piece of paper or in your phone and try to memorize it. Repeat or re-read this verse to yourself when you are struggling to find peace and trust in God in a given moment.

Intermediate

Re-read the section, "Peace Destroyers and Builders for Spiritual Leadership." Try to focus on eliminating one of the "destroyers" that is affecting your peace by replacing it with a peace "builder" this week or month.

Advanced

Visit the adoration chapel in your church each week, spending time with the Lord face to face in prayerful conversation and in silence. This will do more to cultivate peace in you than perhaps anything else. If possible, sign up for a designated hour of adoration to help keep your commitment firm.

8

Becoming the Leader God Made You to Be

"A family is holy
not because it is perfect
but because God's grace is at work
in it, helping it to set out anew every day
on the way of love."
—The United States Conference of Catholic Bishops,
Follow the Way of Love

Placing Everything in the Hands of God

I'll never forget a woman I met during my travels to speak to a group of Catholics about evangelizing young people. She had the kind of comforting presence that made me feel like I was speaking to my own grandmother. Reaching into her stylish, gem-laden handbag, she took out a slightly crumpled picture of her large family. From what I remember, she had about a dozen adult children with several grandchildren. With a twinkle in her eye, she spoke about her son's ordination to the priesthood and what a treasure it was for many of his siblings to be there to witness it in Rome. I asked her if all of her children were practicing Catholics, and with a deep sense of gratitude and humility, she nodded yes.

"Praise God," I told her. "That is a wonderful blessing for you as a mother and a sign not only of God's grace, but of the strength of your spiritual leadership in your family. What was your secret?" I asked her.

"Oh, I placed them all in God's hands a long time ago," she replied, gently shaking her head as if to diminish any compliment I was paying to her. "Every child, everything, in God's hands."

We would be fooling ourselves if we thought that we could become strong spiritual leaders, marching our families to heaven by some formulaic execution of the fundamental characteristics of spiritual leadership mentioned in this book. There is something more that we have to do, perhaps the most fundamental thing, the simplest, and yet the most important thing, and that's to place everything—our marriages, our children, our spiritual lives and our spiritual leadership—entirely in the hands of God.

This remarkable woman I met years ago did not just passively do this, however. It's not as if she just said, "Okay, God, make my family holy," and then sat back and let her family life unravel, somewhat miraculously discovering a happy resolution. She was an active—a very active—participant in God's plan for her and for her family life. She was highly intentional. She placed her leadership in God's hands, effectively saying, "Okay, now *you* lead *me* in this effort. You guide me and my leadership, so I can, in turn, guide and lead my family toward you."

If we entrust our families to the Sacred Heart of Jesus and to the Immaculate Heart of Mary, and then actively pursue the path that the Lord is leading us on, there is no goal too lofty for us. It is the surest path to sainthood, for each of us individually and for those whom God has entrusted to our care.

Not Ours

In the first chapter of the first book of Samuel, a woman, Hannah, painfully weeps as she prays to God about her infertility. "O Lord of hosts," Hannah cries out, "if you will indeed look on the affliction of your maidservant, and . . . will give to your maidservant a son, then I will give him to the Lord all the days of his life" (v. 11).

Hannah recognizes that she is God's mere maidservant, that any child He gives her is really only lent to her from her Creator. When God hears Hannah's prayer and she bears a son, Samuel, she promises, "I will bring him, that he may appear in the presence of the Lord, and abide there for ever" (v. 22). And she does. Hannah goes to the house of God in Shiloh, and proclaims, "For this child I prayed; and the Lord has granted me my petition which I made to him. Therefore I have lent him to the Lord; as long as he lives, he is lent to the Lord" (vv. 27–28). God lent Samuel to Hannah, and then Hannah does the one thing all great spiritual leaders must do: she lends him back to God.

The story goes on to say, "The boy Samuel continued to grow both in stature and in favor with the Lord and with men" (2:26). God makes Samuel into a great and loved prophet, a selfless leader held in high regard by both God and the people of Samuel's day. This is the fruit of strong spiritual leadership. Hannah's recognition that Samuel was not solely hers, but the Lord's, and her entrusting of Samuel to God's care enabled Samuel to become a strong spiritual leader, a powerful instrument of God. Isn't this what we want for ourselves and for our children? One of the greatest gifts we can give our families as spiritual leaders is to lend them to the Lord, for when our families are His, and not ours, something truly magnificent comes of our lives.

Turning Drifting Youth into Strong Spiritual Leaders

This book was written in hopes of opening the floodgates to an abundance of blessings in your personal life—more focus and intentionality, greater mission and peace, more joy and thanksgiving, a stronger marriage and deeper relationship with the Lord. But I also hope that this book will encourage you to better disciple and better lead those in your care, so as to stem the tide of youth drifting away from faith—especially your own children.

Refocusing on your spiritual leadership not only impacts you, but it profoundly influences your children and their own spiritual lives and futures. Mark Hart, who has four children with his wife Melanie, is affectionately known in the Catholic world as "The Bible Geek." As the executive vice president of Life Teen, Mark has focused his entire career on working with and ministering to teens and young adults. Even though Mark spends a significant amount of time equipping parishes to provide excellent catechesis to teens, he wholeheartedly believes that the primary responsibility for handing on the faith, and the place where observing faith has the maximal impact on young people, is in the home.

"When we leave it to others to hand on faith to our children, it sends a painful and dangerous message—either 'I don't understand the faith and I don't need to' or 'This isn't important enough for me to make primary,'" Mark explained. "Both of these scenarios are problematic."

Mark elaborated that "this concept of 'I'll drop off Johnny at 7 pm for faith formation and you can take it from there' is one of the greatest reasons for the massive exodus of Catholics that we have seen for a couple of generations, now." He believes that a turnaround is needed among parents and spiritual leaders today, which involves looking back toward one's marriage vows. "As married couples, we need to reflect—once again—on what we vowed in our wedding ceremony. We pledged that 'if the Lord sends us children,' that we would 'raise them according to the law of Christ and His Church.' Nowhere does it say that we ought to make it 'their choice,' nor does it mention 'convenience' or 'busyness' or 'tantrums,' nor any other reason employed by parents to excuse themselves from their vows. Do my kids always want to go to Mass? No. Are they on the edge of their seat the entire time? No. Do I take them anyway? Yes . . . because that is what love does, it points others to God with every breath. Love works for the salvation of others."

The Harts don't just believe this because of the youth ministry work that they do; they practice what they preach in their own home, making demonstrating a relationship with Christ central in their models of spiritual leadership within their family. "Nothing else I do for the Church matters if my family does not know and feel the love of God through me. My family deserves my primary attention, intercession, and heart," Mark said. As so many other spiritual heads and hearts in this book confess, they, too, uphold that more is caught than taught when it comes to handing on faith to their children.

"The kids can be taught about ritual (like the Mass)," Mark enumerated, "But they need to *see* the relationship we have with the Lord. Growing up, my own father dutifully took us all to Mass each week, but rarely spoke of the Lord. This left me seeking my own relationship with Jesus." Melanie had a different childhood faith background, Mark continued. "Her faith formation came from Baptist and Methodist grandmothers. She had been introduced to Jesus and had a personal relationship with Him. Years later, when she and her family came into the Catholic Church, she was then introduced to this deeper, mystical world of the sacraments."

Mark and Melanie's unique spiritual upbringings ultimately fostered a firm resolve to help nurture in their own children a personal connection with the Lord, the Blessed Mother, and the saints on a daily basis, in addition to helping the Mass and the celebrations of the Church become powerful and meaningful activities in their spiritual lives.

"There is no greater gift, challenge, or honor than to introduce your children to the Lord who entrusted them to you," Mark noted. "Every failure is an invitation to improve, and every success hallows through the halls of heaven. If we want to pass on the faith to our kids, we need time and space to do that. If we really want to bless our children, it will not be merely by including them in our earthly wills and trust funds, but by introducing them to the will of our heavenly Father."

Story of a Family

Since her death on September 30, 1897, St. Thérèse of Lisieux, the Little Flower, continues to capture hearts with her unique simplicity of faith and her small sacrifices made with tremendous love. In learning about her beautiful life, it can be easy to overlook one of the gems of her story: her family background. Sweet Thérèse was not a rose among thorns; she was actually the daughter of tremendously holy parents and one of five faith-filled daughters.

The Martin family was a living witness of the power of self-sacrificial love for God and for others within the home. Zélie and Louis Martin, Thérèse's mother and father, created an environment of holiness within their household, attended daily Mass, and selflessly served one another and the children as they intentionally shared their prayer lives and their Catholic faith. Louis and Zélie, the spiritual head and heart of the Martin family, expected that they and their children pursue heaven with all their might. Fittingly, they were the first married couple to be canonized together in October 2015. All five of their earthly daughters—Thérèse the youngest among them—entered religious life, freely choosing to wed themselves to the Lord in their vocations. The Martins demonstrated the inherent greatness of what family life was created to be.

Writing this book has been a powerful reminder for me that the greatest thing I can do for my spouse and for my children is to become the person that God created me to be. If I become that person, then I will be in the best position to raise a family of saints, to truly give my family all of the spiritual tools they need to grow up loving the Lord and radically living their Christian faith. That's why Louis and Zélie Martin were great parents. They may not have made every little nuanced parenting decision perfectly, but they intensely pursued their own sanctity, which became a source of deep inspiration and transformation for one another and for their children. Becoming the spiritual leader and the saint that God desires you to be is unquestionably the greatest gift that you can give your family.

Examination of Spiritual Leadership

One of the most important practices in the spiritual life is the daily examen, the regular examination of one's conscience, by which you recall your own sins and failings, ask for God's forgiveness, and resolve to avoid those sins in the future. This is a very impactful nighttime activity to add to your routine if you are not in the habit of examining your conscience before you go to bed already.

I recommend that anyone serious about becoming a stronger spiritual leader should do regular examinations of spiritual leadership, too. Consider reviewing this list nightly, weekly, or monthly, taking notes, and evaluating with God, in prayer, and with your spouse, in discussion. I have also included an Examination of Spiritual Leadership bookmark cutout at the back of the book for your convenient use.

- How am I fulfilling my unique and complementary role as the spiritual head/heart of my family?
- Am I working as a balanced team with my spouse in our spiritual leadership of the family?
- What have I done to strengthen my marriage today/this week/this month?
- Have I prioritized prayer today/this week/this month?
- What does my prayer life look like right now?
- Is our home, the domestic church, reminiscent of the larger Church?
- Am I praying, evangelizing, and participating regularly in the sacraments?
- What have I done to grow in virtue today/this week/this month?
- Which virtues am I lacking in?
- How have I infused my family life with Catholic culture today/this week/this month?
- Have I read about, discussed, or prayed with the life of a saint or the stories in Scripture?
- Have I celebrated a feast day recently or prepared my family to receive the Eucharist with reverence and anticipation?
- How have I handled the little or large crosses that have come my way today/this week/this month?
- Am I offering up my sufferings?
- What have I done today/this week/this month to learn more about my faith?
- What have I done today/this week/this month to teach something about my faith to my family?
- How, concretely, have I cultivated peace today/this week/this month, in my heart and in my home?
- How am I living up to, and helping my family live up to, our family mission?

Once you review and take mental or written (strongly recommended) note of your progress in these areas, make a plan to improve, even if you focus on improving in just *one* of these areas the following day, week, or month. Recruit your spouse or your faith group that you are going through this book with as accountability partners to encourage you and motivate you in your resolution to become a stronger spiritual leader and examine your progress regularly.

Lastly, you may also like to turn to the words of St. Paul to the Romans at the end of this examination. His reflections on the marks of a true Christian motivate me to begin anew each day and pursue with greater fervor my role as the spiritual heart of my family. "Never flag in zeal, be aglow with the Spirit, serve the Lord. Rejoice in your hope, be patient in tribulation, be constant in prayer" (12:11–12).

By Way of the Family

I wrote this book not only for you, as the reader, to become a stronger spiritual leader for your family, but so that my husband and I could have a plan for intentionally leading our own family toward heaven. This project has been transformative for us, but our work has really only just begun. I envision that the strong spiritual leaders I interviewed in this book will be regular companions on our own leadership journeys, and that the action steps and reflections provided in each chapter will be referenced repeatedly, sometimes more frequently than others, as we start to slip in certain characteristics of our leadership that need a little fixing, or as we seek to advance toward deeper ways of practicing our spiritual leadership in the areas where we have made good progress.

I also expect that, being complementary to one another, we'll likely have times when we are working on different characteristics. For example, I'll probably be in a perpetual state of trying to lead my family toward greater peace as I try to fight stress in my personal life, while my husband may spend more time focusing his energy on another area of leadership. For the sake of accountability, I suggested to my husband that we ask each other every night before bed, "What have you done to become a stronger spiritual leader today?" This is a simple and helpful way to connect with one another at the end of the evening, briefly examine your own leadership, and encourage each other to grow. If you are not able to complete the full Examination of Spiritual Leadership mentioned above on a nightly basis, do this instead, and use the full examination weekly or monthly.

Spiritual leadership is a lifelong process, a journey of coming closer and closer to what it means to be and to live out our roles as the spiritual head and spiritual heart of our growing family. First, I prayed about this book. Then, I wrote it. Now the real challenge comes: living it, and living it not just for a day or for a year, but from now until the day I encounter my Lord in heaven, eagerly anticipating the words, "Well done, good and faithful servant. Well done; you became the spiritual leader I made you to be."

As we near the end of our lives, so much of what we do will fade into the background of the time that we spend here on earth, but, God willing, one thing will always remain paramount in importance: our family. Pope St. John Paul II said, "Humanity passes by way of the family" (*Familiaris Consortio*, 86). For those of us called to spiritual leadership in family life, I think a life well lived also passes by way of the family. How we respond to our call to live out the Gospel in our own homes, to grow in holiness in some small way as an individual, as a couple, and as a family every day, impacts the joy and meaning with which we paint our days. This spiritual leadership of our families—becoming the spiritual heads and hearts God made us to be—is what we were created for.

Epilogue

Spiritual Leaders Learn and Teach the Faith

Strong spiritual leaders know the colossal impact they have on their children's current and future faith practice. Setting an example of faithful discipleship is paramount in their handing on the Gospel and leading their family toward a fruitful relationship with Christ. Also important is their dedication to *speaking* what they believe. Many of our young people do not have a language with which they can express their faith. They are uncomfortable with verbal evangelization, in large part because their parents don't do it and never taught them how to do it themselves. Fortunately, this problem can be remedied, starting in the home. It begins with simple conversation about faith between spouses and between parents and children. When families practice talking about their spiritual journeys, about the core beliefs of their faith, the messages of Scripture, the doctrines and practices of the Church, and the ways in which Christ is working in their lives, a language of faith is developed that spiritual leaders and their children will have for the rest of their lives. This language becomes a basis for which they both learn and teach the faith in and outside of the home.

As the spiritual leaders of your family, you are the *primary* educators of your children—not the pastor, not the youth minister, not the Sunday school catechist, Confirmation coordinator, or Catholic school theology teacher. *You and your spouse* have the privilege and the responsibility to teach your children about their Christian faith, which also requires that you continually learn about it yourself. One of the hallmarks of strong spiritual leadership is the ability to be a continuous student and teacher of the Catholic faith, first and foremost in the home and among the family.

To assist you in your endeavor to become a better student and teacher of the Catholic faith, I have included this helpful introductory list of resources. For a more extensive listing of resources, separated by learning subject and type of resource (online, book, audio/visual, or study program), I encourage you to visit my website, CatholicKatie.com, where you can access my free *Catholic Resource Guide for Spiritual Leaders*, with hundreds of resources to help you better learn and teach the Catholic faith.

The essentials: The Bible, *The Catechism of the Catholic Church*, and YOUCAT. Start here! If you don't have these books, or you have them for decorative purposes only, get them from your local Catholic bookstore or from your coffee table, dust them off, and begin reading. As for Bible translations, I probably most frequently read from the Ignatius Revised Standard Version Second Catholic Edition. Read a helpful narrative with your Bible, like Jeff Cavins and Dr. Tim Gray's *Walking With God*, to help you unpack the stories of Scripture, or download an app like *Opening the Word* that aids in your biblical reflection. Along with your Catechism, grab a great compendium or explanatory text, like Dr. Peter Kreeft's *Catholic Christianity: A Complete Catechism of Catholic Beliefs Based on the Catechism of the Catholic Church*.

The spiritual classics: There are scores of classic spiritual masterpieces from the saints of the past that are a great launching point for your spiritual leadership. Dr. Ralph Martin of Renewal Ministries has compiled much of the wisdom of these saints in his work, *The Fulfillment of All Desire: A Guidebook for the Journey to God Based on the Wisdom of the Saints* (Emmaus Road Publishing).

The modern greats: We have so many amazing Catholic authors in the Church today that there are too many to name here. Go to a Catholic bookstore or website you trust and pick up a book that is of interest to you. Commit to reading an educational book at least once a year. For example, consider reading a book to improve your marriage (strengthening the third spiritual leadership characteristic mentioned in the book) by Dr. Gregory Popcak, a Catholic psychotherapist and author with an arsenal of practical and inspiring books to help you become a better spouse.

The Catholic blogosphere: Evangelization and Catholic learning tools have expanded rapidly on the Internet. You can now read fantastic blog posts and acquire all sorts of helpful resources from Catholic bloggers, some of whom are contributors to this book. (Look them up! For example, Matthew Warner, contributor to the chapter on prayer, is the man behind the curtain of one of my favorite blogs, RadicalLife.org.)

Top Catholic websites: I regularly promote my favorite learning and teaching resources on the websites I write for and get many of my own learning tools from: CatholicsComeHome.org, IntegratedCatholicLife.org, and NCRegister.com. I'm also a regular visitor to Catholic.com and CatholicEducation.org. You can't visit these websites without learning a lot about your faith. CatholicAllYear.com and CatholicIcing.com will help you craftily and creatively teach your kids the faith, too.

Catholic TV, radio, and podcasts: Catholic TV and radio programming is an often-hidden gem to many Catholics today, but it will help your spiritual leadership immensely. I love watching or listening live on the Internet, or downloading my favorite podcasts from radio shows on EWTN, Ave Maria, and Immaculate Heart radio stations, for example.

Faith-building programs: My recent favorite is the Augustine Institute's *Symbolon* program, which helps you "discover the big picture of the Catholic faith . . . and how to live it." It's a great DVD series to go through with your spouse or with others in your faith community. A few other programs or faith building projects to look into include: *The Great Adventure* Bible Study series, *That Man is You*, WINE: *Women in the New Evangelization (Catholic Vineyard)*, *Blessed Is She*, and *Legatus,* an organization where Catholic business leaders and their spouses can become "ambassadors for Christ."

Parish ministries: Participate in the adult faith formation opportunities your parish has to offer, and volunteer as a catechist for the younger catechesis programs (like Sunday school, or First Communion or Confirmation prep). Your parish ministries offer you great opportunities to both learn and teach the faith.

My website, CatholicKatie.com: What I love even more than great resources is sharing top-notch resources with others. Visit my website or join my email list for access to many of my favorite tools for studying and teaching the faith.

Appendix

A Quick Reference Prayer List from the Church's Treasury of Prayers

Wondering where to start in personal or family prayer? Here is a quick, go-to list of some of the many favorite prayers and prayer traditions that aspiring spiritual leaders use in their personal, spousal, and family prayer lives.

- The Mass
- The Rosary (and the individual prayers it contains: the Creed, Our Father, Hail Mary, Glory Be, Fatima Prayer, Hail Holy Queen)
- The "Jesus" prayer (reciting the name of Jesus)
- Grace before meals (and even after meals, too)
- Prayer to your Guardian Angel
- The Divine Mercy Chaplet
- The Angelus
- The Memorare
- The Act of Contrition and the Daily Examen
- Prayer to St. Michael the Archangel
- Novenas (endless options for almost every need, celebration, and saint!)
- Lectio divina (a wonderful way to pray with Scripture)
- The Psalms

- The Liturgy of the Hours (also known as the Divine Office)
- Meditation
- Eucharistic Adoration
- Spontaneous prayer ("Thank you, Jesus!," "Lord, please grant me patience in this moment," "God, please come to the aid of whomever that ambulance is for," etc.)
- Silence (what I like to call "golden prayer," just "being" with Jesus). Mother Teresa wrote, "Our prayer life suffers so much because our hearts are not silent," and Scripture reminds us, "Be still, and know that I am God" (Ps 46:10).

About the Author

Katie Warner is a wife, stay-at-home mother, author, speaker, and evangelist who helps inspire and practically guide others to take small steps toward more meaningful and spiritual lives.

Katie is a correspondent for the *National Catholic Register* and one of the original contributing writers for the *Integrated Catholic Life*. As a speaker, her joyful, down-to-earth and engaging manner of presentation has captivated audiences around the country. She has made multiple appearances on EWTN television and is a guest on Catholic radio.

Katie works part-time as the Manager of Communication and Evangelization for the media apostolate *Catholics Come Home*, and as a segment host for the popular TV series *Catholics Come Home*. She holds a graduate degree in Theology from the Augustine Institute, and is a presenter for the Augustine Institute's acclaimed *Symbolon* and *Opening the Word* faith formation programs.

Katie's favorite ministry work is family life, where she relishes every day that she spends loving, laughing, playing, and praying with her spouse and son.

Contact the Author

If this book has impacted you or your family in some way, please share with me; I'd love to hear from you. I also have additional resources for your spiritual leadership journey available through my website. You can reach me at CatholicKatie.com or through social media, on Twitter @CatholicKatie and on my author Facebook page (search: "Katie Warner").

May God bless you as you become the spiritual leader God created you to be.

Examination of Spiritual Leadership

I recommend that you do this spiritual leadership examen daily, but reviewing the list weekly or monthly will also help you grow as the spiritual head or spiritual heart of your family.

Begin in prayer. Pray any words from your heart or this prayer: "Lord, please open my eyes to see the ways that I am effectively leading my family and to discover the areas where I need to improve. With your grace, help me to become the spiritual leader that you desire me to be."

Ask yourself:
- How am I fulfilling my unique and complementary role as the spiritual head/heart of my family?
- Am I working as a balanced team with my spouse in our spiritual leadership of the family?
- How have I strengthened my marriage today/this week/this month?
- Have I prioritized prayer today/this week/this month?
- Is our home, the domestic church, reminiscent of the larger Church?
- Am I praying, evangelizing, and participating in the sacraments?
- What have I done to grow in virtue today/this week/this month?
- Which virtues am I lacking?
- Have I infused my family life with Catholic culture today/this week/this month?
- Have I prepared my family to receive the Eucharist with reverence?
- How have I handled the little or large crosses that have come my way today/this week/this month?
- Am I offering up my sufferings?
- How have I cultivated peace today/this week/this month, in my heart and in my home?
- What have I done today/this week/this month to learn more about my faith?
- How am I living up to, and helping my family fulfill our mission?

Make a plan to improve and discuss with your spouse. Select one thing to focus on improving and choose steps to take to ensure progress. Rely on your spouse as an accountability partner, teammate, motivator, and encourager.

End in prayer. End with a heartfelt prayer or these words: "Dear Jesus, through the intercession of the Blessed Mother and St. Joseph, I ask you to give me grace and fervor to fulfill my role as a spiritual leader in a joyful, intentional way. I love you, thank you, and praise you for this awesome responsibility of leading my family toward heaven. Amen."

QUEEN MOTHER

EDWARD SRI

— General Editor —
SCOTT HAHN

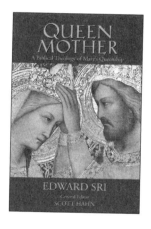

Queen Mother explores the role of the queen mother in the Davidic kingdom, examining the ways in which this theme sheds light on Mary's role as heavenly Queen and Mother of the Church. As he proceeds through the New Testament, Dr. Sri demonstrates the ultimate convergence of the queen-mother theme in the Gospels and the Book of Revelation.

978-1-931018-24-1 // paperback
978-1-63446-018-7 // hardbound

....

"The biblical queen-mother tradition is of paramount importance for our contemporary understanding of Our Lady's dynamic role of spiritual queen and advocate for all humanity. Edward Sri offers an outstanding synthesis of this *Gebirah* or 'Great Lady' biblical revelation."

—MARK MIRAVALLE, S.T.D. Professor of Theology,
Franciscan University of Steubenville

"This book intelligently deepens one's devotion to Mary, the Queen of Heaven, the Mother of Jesus, and the Mother of the Church."

—REV. JOSEPH HENCHEY, C.S.S. Professor Emeritus,
Pontifical North American College, Rome

emmausroad.org • (800) 398-5470

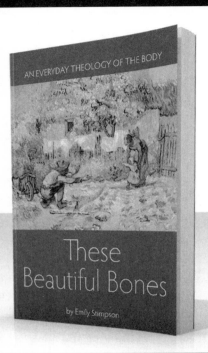

A PRACTICAL AND FAITHFUL
GUIDE TO MARRIAGE

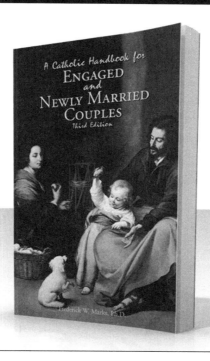

A Catholic Handbook for
ENGAGED AND NEWLY MARRIED COUPLES
DR. FREDERICK W. MARKS

This guide to marriage is outstanding both for its practicality and for its fidelity to the Catholic Faith, showing us the secrets of building a sound, spiritual relationship with your fiancé or spouse—from toothpaste in the sink to natural family planning. It offers suggestions on most aspects of married life, such as the wedding, the honeymoon, the relationship between husband and wife, in-laws, finances, raising children, sexual relations, practicing the faith, and developing a spiritual life of personal relations with God.

It also offers excellent advice on how to live the Catholic faith as a married man or woman. Dr. Marks spells out clearly what the Catholic Church expects of married people in the areas of married life, sexuality, and family life.

EMMAUS
ROAD
PUBLISHING

Call **(800) 398-5470** to order
or visit **EmmausRoad.org**

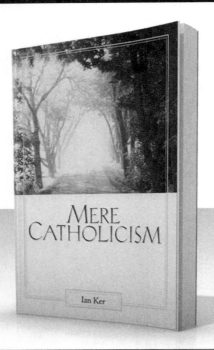